AWESOME
Science Experiments
for Kids

AWESOME SCIENCE EXPERIMENTS for Kids

100+ FUN S T E A M PROJECTS AND WHY THEY WORK!

CRYSTAL CHATTERTON

Photography by Paige Green

ROCKRIDGE PRESS

SAFETY NOTE: All of the experiments in this book are intended to be performed under adult supervision. Appropriate and reasonable caution is required at all times, and the recommendations in the activities in this book cannot replace common and sound judgment. Observe safety and caution at all times. The author and Publisher disclaim all liability for any damage, mishap, or injury that may occur from engaging in the activities featured in this book.

For general information on our other products and services or to obtain technical support, please contact our Customer Care Department within the United States at (866) 744-2665, or outside the United States at (510) 253-0500.

Rockridge Press publishes its books in a variety of electronic and print formats. Some content that appears in print may not be available in electronic books, and vice versa.

Photographs © 2018 by Paige Green
Styling by Alysia Andriola

ISBN: Print 978-1-93975-466-0
eBook 978-1-93975-467-7

For my three mini scientists,

Tommy, Lily, and Clara, whose inquisitive questions
and thirst for answers inspired the experiments
and activities in this book.

Contents

Introduction

Welcome to *Awesome Science Experiments for Kids*!

In this book you will find 105 fun projects that will surprise, delight, and teach kids ages 5 to 10. The book is divided into chapters that cover each of the following important areas: **S**cience, **T**echnology, **E**ngineering, **A**rt, and **M**ath. Together we call this **STEAM**.

I have been passionate about science and math my entire life. After earning a master's degree in organic chemistry and working in a laboratory, I started my own family of mini scientists who are now ages 8, 6, and 2. In 2012, I launched my blog, *The Science Kiddo*, and have been working ever since to share hundreds of easy kids' science experiments with thousands of parents and educators around the world.

A few years ago, the buzzword in the field of education was *STEM*. You may be familiar with this term. However, as art and design have become increasingly important and we have realized the intricate interplay between the arts and the sciences, the A for *art* was added to create *STEAM*.

All of these fields are connected to one another in numerous ways. Designing a structure involves elements of art and engineering. Making a robot involves knowledge of technology, engineering, and science. Being able to measure the results of any science experiment involves the principles of math.

This book is designed to be like real life by showing the interplay among all of the STEAM fields. Scientists working in a laboratory need to accurately calculate and measure materials and record results. They not only need to have intimate knowledge of science, but they also need to possess the creativity and ingenuity to design and invent pathways that did not previously exist.

Likewise, electrical engineers don't just create circuits on a control panel. They need to know the physics behind the circuitry, be familiar with the technology available, design and build new models, and be able to measure the output. All of the STEAM fields contribute to the engineers' successes.

The experiments in this book are, above everything else, loads of fun. Whether you are an adult or a kid, you will learn new things and do experiments that will make you throw your hands up and cheer. You will have opportunities to build on the simple principles to create more impressive and more creative results. And, best of all, you will be able to do most of this with materials you already have at home or can easily and inexpensively find at the store.

A few materials, such as alligator-clip wires and LEDs required for experiments in the technology chapter, may have to be purchased online or at an electronics store. But don't worry—these materials are inexpensive and easy to find. For ease, I have listed special materials needed for each chapter in their respective introduction.

In each chapter, you will find experiments that are simply and clearly outlined. Each experiment includes a list of materials and easy-to-read, step-by-step instructions.

Each experiment also outlines a few observation questions to get kids thinking more deeply about what they are seeing. An extension activity is provided at the end of each experiment as well, designed to build on the principles at work. This is where children's true creativity shines as they create new experiments based on the observations and new questions they have.

Most of the experiments are designed to be done as an adult-and-child team, but older kids may find that they can do many of the experiments completely on their own.

The most useful feature of this book is *The Hows and Whys* section at the end of each experiment. This section explains in simple terms what is going on at a molecular level to make the experiment happen the way it does. Kids can use this knowledge to build on what they have learned and invent their own science experiments.

At the end of the book you will find a glossary filled with vocabulary words and terms that budding scientists need to know, along with blank table and graph pages. These will come in handy for many of the experiments in the math chapter as children measure and record their results. Feel free to make as many photocopies as needed of these pages.

Awesome Science Experiments for Kids is an interactive book, designed to teach kids how to think and create like real scientists by using the scientific method. The techniques of the scientific method have been used since the seventeenth century to investigate phenomena and acquire new knowledge. Perhaps you are already familiar with these steps of the scientific method:

- Ask a question
- Do background research
- Formulate a hypothesis
- Design an experiment
- Test the hypothesis
- Analyze the data
- Draw a conclusion

Each of these steps is important. This book is designed to walk kids through the entire scientific method, first with well-designed instructions, and then with additional questions and ideas to extend their scientific thinking skills.

In each experiment, children are asked a question and given a small introduction. It is up to them to formulate a hypothesis, or an educated guess, about what will happen during the experiment. At the end, they will draw conclusions from what they observed to see if their hypothesis was correct.

These experiments are meant to be used as a springboard into asking more questions and designing bigger and better experiments that answer those questions. The art of asking a question and designing an experiment to find the answer is what makes experiments what they are. Without a question, an experiment is just a demonstration—a recipe that will produce a cool result, but without the deep thinking and learning that comes when questions are asked and answered. Adults are encouraged to ask kids questions and discover the answers together. Use this book not only as an amazing learning tool but also as a fun bonding experience that kids will treasure.

By understanding the principles of STEAM, a child will be set up for success in life. Yes, there are thousands of new jobs opening up in these fields each year that need qualified and creative people to fill them, but that's not really the point. The point is that learning to question, design, build, create, measure, and think critically will set a child up for astounding success in whatever educational and vocational fields he or she chooses to pursue. Plus, STEAM is loads of fun!

Happy learning!

Chapter One

HOW TO USE THIS BOOK

The experiments in this book are divided into chapters by each category of STEAM: **Science**, Technology, **E**ngineering, **A**rt, and **M**ath. However, since all of these fields overlap and connect, many of the experiments could fit into multiple categories. You will find a color-coded tab on each experiment that makes it easy to identify other STEAM categories the experiment could fit into. The index also lists this interchangeability in one easy-to-find location. At the end of the book, you will also find a Resources section with STEAM-related websites. These are provided for further discovery and enrichment.

Let's dive into the heart of the book: the experiments!

GETTING READY

There are so many fun and interesting experiments to choose from in this book! They all work independently, so you can pick and choose which ones to do and in what order. No need to start with the first one or complete them in order as they appear. Choose a time to sit down together as an adult-and-child team to decide which experiments look the most fun and interesting to you and go from there.

Once you have decided which experiment to start with, look ahead at the list of materials to see what you need to gather. Most of the supplies used in this book are things you probably already have at home. However, if you don't have everything on the list, make a plan to run to the store to pick up the items you need.

Make sure to have a notebook and a pencil ready. Effective scientists keep detailed notes, write down their questions, draw pictures, record their observations, and track their results. Get into these good habits now so that you can maximize your learning and fun.

When you have all of the materials you need, sit down together and read *The Big Question*. This section introduces the experiment and asks a question or two to get the wheels rolling. Think about other questions you may have that are related to the same topic and write them down.

Once you are familiar with what the experiment is about, formulate a hypothesis. This is an educated guess, or a statement of what you think will happen during the experiment. You may already be familiar with the experiment and know what will happen. That's just fine. State a hypothesis anyway and double-check that you are right. This is what scientists do.

A hypothesis follows the format, "I think . . . because . . ." It's not a random guess. It's an educated statement. Think through what you already know. Have a reason behind your guess.

For example, if you are mixing baking soda and vinegar together, a hypothesis may be "*I think* an eruption will happen because lots of bubbles are produced." Doing the experiment will confirm whether your hypothesis is correct.

Guess what? It's totally fine if your hypothesis is incorrect. Some of the experiments in this book are very surprising and may produce a result you aren't expecting! Often the most gratifying fun and learning come with an unexpected outcome. Being wrong and making mistakes open up the door for more questions to be asked and more answers to be discovered.

Glance over the level of difficulty and the time required for the experiment to make sure it suits your needs. Most of the experiments are quick, with immediate results, but a few take some time to develop.

Last, be sure to read the *Caution* section for each experiment, if it has one. Some of the experiments are quite fun but messy and should be done outside. Sometimes a child might need an adult's help with a tool or might need to stand back a few feet. Be aware of anything that could be a potential hazard.

Once you are all set up, roll up your sleeves and get ready to have fun!

DOING THE EXPERIMENT

Easy, step-by-step instructions are outlined for each experiment. Carefully follow the instructions to complete the experiment and note any variations you make.

After the experiment is complete, take some time to read and answer the questions in the *Observations* section. Was your hypothesis correct? What surprising or interesting things did you notice during the experiment? Why do you think you got a particular outcome? Write down your answers and note further questions you have.

Be sure to read *The Hows and Whys* section of each experiment. This is where the science behind what you see is explained in simple terms. It makes the science in our world come to life!

There are lots of scientific terms in this book that new scientists need to learn. Unfamiliar words are defined in the glossary at the back of the book. Use the Internet or the dictionary to research additional unfamiliar terms.

Additional ideas for experimenting are suggested in the *Now Try This!* section. This is where all of your knowledge comes together, and you can design and complete further experiments on your own. Use what you learned during the experiment to ask more questions and to design and complete new experiments.

Because the elements of STEAM are so interconnected, many of the experiments can fall under several different categories. For example, launching projectiles with a catapult requires knowledge of potential and kinetic energy (science), familiarity with simple machines (technology), a clear idea of how to build it (engineering), creative thinking to design it (art), and a way to measure how far the projectiles fly (math). These fields are intimately related. Where relevant, the different categories are noted at the beginning of the experiment and highlighted in the icons at the bottom of the page.

Remember not to be discouraged if the experiment doesn't work the way it is *supposed* to. Failure is an opportunity to learn and discover new things. Troubleshoot the experiment, change some variables, and try again. And the best part about these experiments is that despite the result, adults and children alike will have fun!

Chapter Two

SCIENCE

Be prepared to create and discover amazing things!

In this chapter, you will inflate a balloon without blowing into it, create a rainbow rainstorm, pop a plastic baggie with a simple chemical reaction, dissolve the shell right off of an egg, grow an overnight crystal garden, and much, much more!

Almost all of the supplies required for the experiments in this chapter are things you probably already have at home. However, there are two special supplies you may need to purchase. To conduct the Foam Explosion experiment (page 36) you will need ½ cup of 20 volume (6%) hydrogen peroxide. This can be purchased at a beauty supply store or online for about $3. The other specialty supply is about 3 feet of vinyl tubing for the Soda Can Submarine experiment (page 60). This can be found inexpensively at a hardware store or online.

As a budding scientist, there are a few guidelines you should keep in mind for performing science experiments.

First, always ask questions. Lots and lots of questions. The difference between a boring science experiment and an exciting one is whether you are asking the right questions. Be sure to ask "Why does this happen?" and "How does this work?" often.

Second, take the questions you have and experiment further. The science experiments in this chapter are a starting point to a lifelong pursuit of asking questions and designing experiments to find answers to those questions.

Third, failure is a step in the right direction. If an experiment doesn't work the way it's supposed to, ask yourself why and learn from it.

Troubleshoot and change some variables. In a real laboratory, scientists learn what doesn't work more often than they learn what does work. It's all knowledge and it's all in the right direction. Don't get discouraged.

Fourth, keep track of your results. Grab a notebook and write down the experiments you have done and what you have learned. Write down your questions and your ideas for further experimentation. Draw pictures. If you change a variable, keep track of what you altered and what the result was. Good scientists keep meticulous notes.

And last, have a ton of fun. Learning and discovering new things is one of the most gratifying experiences you can have in life. Take pleasure in the surprises and remember the "Aha!" moments.

DANCING RAISINS

LEVEL OF DIFFICULTY: EASY
FROM BEGINNING TO END: 10 MINUTES

? What do you think will happen when raisins are added to a cup of clear carbonated soda? Will they sink? Will they float? The results may surprise you, but you'll be rewarded with a sweet snack at the end.

MATERIALS

- 2 clear cups
- Clear carbonated soda
- Water
- Raisins

THE STEPS

1. Pour soda into one of the cups and water into the other cup. The cup of water is your scientific control.

2. Add a few raisins to each cup one by one.

Observations How do the raisins in the cup of water compare with the raisins in the soda?

Now Try This! What other small objects do you think will dance in soda? Some ideas to try include beads, other dried fruit, corn kernels, lentil beans, and dried pasta.

The Hows and Whys Tiny bubbles of carbon dioxide in the soda attach to the uneven surface of the raisins. All of the little wrinkles on the raisins provide nucleation sites for the carbon dioxide bubbles. When enough bubbles attach to a raisin, it floats to the top of the cup as if it is wearing hundreds of tiny life preservers. Those bubbles pop at the surface and the raisin floats back down, ready to pick up more bubbles. This creates the effect that they are dancing in the cup!

BALLOON IN A BOTTLE

LEVEL OF DIFFICULTY: MEDIUM
FROM BEGINNING TO END: 20 MINUTES

? What is the relationship between temperature and pressure? In this hands-on science experiment, you will see how pressure changes with temperature while performing a really cool and surprising science trick. Your friends will think you went to Hogwarts!

! *Caution:* **Ask an adult to help you handle hot water and hot glass. Remember that hot glass looks like cold glass and to use oven mitts when handling the glass throughout the duration of the experiment.**

MATERIALS
- Glass bottle with a narrow neck
- Water
- Oven mitts
- Trivet
- Party balloon
- Measuring spoons

THE STEPS

1. Pour 1 tablespoon of water into the bottle.

2. Place the bottle in the microwave and heat for 1 minute. If the bottle is too tall to fit in the microwave, rest it diagonally in another microwave-safe bowl and heat it up that way.

3. The bottle and water will be very hot coming out of the microwave. Use oven mitts to grab the bottle and set it on a trivet on the kitchen counter.

4. With your oven mitts still on, quickly stretch a balloon over the mouth of the bottle. Make sure the balloon is centered over the mouth and sit back to watch what happens next.

Observations What happened to the balloon? What changes did you observe in the bottle after it was removed from the microwave?

Now Try This! How do you think you can push the balloon out of the bottle using the principles taught in this experiment?

The Hows and Whys Temperature and pressure are directly proportional, meaning that when temperature rises, so does pressure. When the water in the bottle is hot, it exerts a lot of pressure. However, as it cools down and the water vapor condenses back into water droplets, the pressure decreases. As it cools, the pressure on the outside of the bottle is greater than the pressure inside the bottle. This creates a vacuum, causing air to push into the bottle from the outside, bringing the balloon along with it.

FALLING ORANGE

LEVEL OF DIFFICULTY: EASY

FROM BEGINNING TO END: 10 MINUTES

? Have you ever seen the trick where someone pulls a tablecloth out from under a bunch of dishes without breaking them? Have you ever wondered how this is possible? Try a similar (and less expensive) trick that will impress your friends and teach them about inertia at the same time.

MATERIALS

- Plastic pitcher filled halfway with water
- Postcard
- Cardboard tube (like a toilet paper roll or paper towel roll)
- Orange

THE STEPS

1. Set up this demonstration by placing a postcard over the top of the pitcher.

2. Stand the cardboard tube on top of the postcard.

3. Balance the orange on top of the cardboard tube so that it is right over the mouth of the pitcher.

4. When you are ready, quickly pull the postcard away and watch what happens.

CONTINUED ➡

Observations What happened to the orange when the postcard was pulled away?

Now Try This! What happens if you leave the cardboard tube out of the experiment and place the orange directly on the postcard? Does it work the same? Why? What happens if you use something heavier than an orange, like a grapefruit or a melon?

The Hows and Whys Newton's first law of motion states, "An object at rest stays at rest and an object in motion stays in motion unless acted upon by an unbalanced force." The tendency of an object to maintain its current state of motion is called inertia.

Objects with more mass have more inertia. In other words, heavier objects resist a change in their motion more than light objects do.

The cardboard tube is light and doesn't have a lot of inertia, while the orange is heavier and has more inertia. Because the orange is much heavier, it isn't moved as easily by the same pull. It stays in the same position and falls directly into the pitcher.

DIVING KETCHUP

LEVEL OF DIFFICULTY: EASY
FROM BEGINNING TO END: 15 MINUTES

? Can you sink an object that naturally floats in water without touching it? Learn a cool science trick while also learning about the relationship between volume and density.

MATERIALS

- Ketchup or mustard packet
- Small bowl full of water
- 2-liter plastic bottle with cap
- Water

THE STEPS

1. Test to make sure your ketchup or mustard packet floats by placing it in a bowl of water. If it sinks, try another packet until you find one that floats.

2. Place a ketchup packet that floats in the bottle.

3. Fill up the bottle to the rim with water and secure the cap.

4. The packet should be floating at the top of the bottle. Grab the bottle with both hands and squeeze as hard as you can.

Observations What happens to the ketchup packet when you squeeze the bottle? What happens when you let go?

Now Try This! Add a few tablespoons of salt to the water in the bottle and try this experiment again. Does salt water change how the ketchup packet behaves?

The Hows and Whys When ketchup and mustard packets are sealed at the factory, a small bubble of air often gets trapped inside. This small bubble is enough to make the entire packet float. However, when the bottle is squeezed, the air inside the packet is compressed into a smaller space, which makes it more dense. The packet sinks to the bottom of the bottle until you release the pressure.

FIZZY ROCKET

LEVEL OF DIFFICULTY: EASY

FROM BEGINNING TO END: 30 MINUTES

Can you launch your own rocket using a common chemical reaction? Learn about pressure and watch what happens when the pressure overcomes the strength of a container.

Caution: Be sure you stand a few feet back from the rockets so you don't get hit when they launch! Do this experiment outside where it's fine to make a little bit of a mess.

MATERIALS

- M&M's Minis candy in the pop-top tube (If you can't find one of these, any small bottle with a lid that snaps on will work. Some vitamin bottles have this; the old 35mm film canisters work the best.)
- Scissors
- Alka-Seltzer tablet
- Water

THE STEPS

1. Head outside where it's fine to make a little mess.

2. Use scissors to cut the small piece of plastic holding the lid to the tube so that the lid comes off freely.

3. Place an Alka-Seltzer tablet in the canister.

4. Fill the tube up about ¾ full with water and pop the lid on. Set the rocket on the ground upside down (on its lid) and step back a few feet.

5. Watch and wait for the rocket to launch!

Observations What happened when the rocket launched? What did you notice before it launched?

Now Try This! Vary the amount of water and the size of the Alka-Seltzer tablet you add to the canister. Does it make a difference in how quickly or how high it launches? How does water temperature affect the rocket?

The Hows and Whys The key to launching this rocket is the chemical reaction that happens when Alka-Seltzer tablets dissolve in water. These tablets are made from a dry acid (citric acid) and a dry base (sodium bicarbonate) that react to form carbon dioxide gas when they dissolve in water. As more and more carbon dioxide is produced, the pressure inside the canister builds until at last the canister is launched off the top!

BEAN IN A BAG

LEVEL OF DIFFICULTY: EASY

FROM BEGINNING TO END: 7 TO 10 DAYS

? What is the effect of sunlight on plant growth? Does a seed in darkness sprout at the same time as a seed in the sunlight? Try this simple experiment to find out.

MATERIALS

- 2 plastic zip-top baggies
- 2 paper towel sheets
- Handful of dry beans (like pinto beans, black beans, navy beans, etc.)

THE STEPS

1. Fold each paper towel so that it fits into a baggie.

2. Saturate the paper towels with water and place one towel into each baggie.

3. Place a few dry beans into each baggie on top of the paper towel and zip up the bags.

4. Carefully place one baggie in a sunny place where it won't be disturbed. Place the other baggie in a dark closet without any sunlight.

5. Check on the beans daily and record your observations.

Observations After 7 to 10 days, how are the beans in each baggie different? How are they similar? On which day did the beans germinate?

Now Try This! Place a third set of beans in a baggie in the refrigerator. Make sure the paper towel stays wet and note how these seeds grow compared with the beans in the closet and the sunny place.

The Hows and Whys Dry beans are simply the seeds of the bean plant. In order for these seeds to sprout, they need warmth, water, and oxygen. A seed in a baggie, whether in darkness or in sunlight, has everything it needs to germinate. However, once the seeds sprout, they do need sunlight to make their food through photosynthesis.

TORNADO IN A BOTTLE

LEVEL OF DIFFICULTY: EASY
FROM BEGINNING TO END: 20 MINUTES
OTHER CATEGORIES: ENGINEERING

 Can you capture a tornado in a bottle? Grab a few quick supplies and get spinning.

MATERIALS

- Two 2-liter plastic bottles
- Water
- Small plastic beads or small wadded up pieces of paper
- Metal washer
- Duct tape

THE STEPS

1. Fill one bottle about ¾ full of water. Add some beads to the bottle. (This will make the tornado easier to see.)

2. Place a metal washer on the lip of the bottle.

3. Position the empty bottle upside down so its mouth is on top of the washer.

4. Use duct tape to secure the bottles together.

5. Flip the bottles over, so that the empty one is on the bottom, and observe what happens.

6. When all the water has drained from the top bottle into the bottom bottle, flip them over again. This time, swirl the bottles in a circular motion and observe what happens.

Observations Which method empties the water from the bottle the fastest?

Now Try This! Experiment to discover the quickest way to transfer all the water from one bottle to another. Shake, squeeze, swirl, or let it sit to find out which method works the best.

The Hows and Whys When you swirl the bottles, it creates a vortex that makes it easier for air to come in and for water to flow out. Without a vortex, the air and water have to take turns flowing through the mouth of the bottle and may even come to pressure equilibrium—where nothing moves.

CORNSTARCH QUICKSAND

LEVEL OF DIFFICULTY: EASY
FROM BEGINNING TO END: 30 MINUTES

? Do you know how quicksand works? It's easy to sink in but extremely difficult to get out of because it hardens when pressure is applied to it. Make your own quick-sand and learn about its unique properties in this super fun and messy science experiment.

! Caution: This experiment can get very messy, depending on how much you get into it! When you are done experimenting and playing, throw the cornstarch mixture away in the trash. It will clog the drain if you try to wash it down the sink.

MATERIALS

- Large mixing bowl
- Cornstarch
- Water
- Food coloring
- Slotted spoon, colander, kitchen sieve, funnel, and other kitchen tools

THE STEPS

1. In a mixing bowl, mix 2 parts cornstarch to 1 part water. For example, if you have 1 cup of cornstarch, mix it with ½ cup water.

2. Add a few drops of food coloring, just for fun. Mix it well.

3. Have fun exploring this mixture. Make a ball of it in your hand and then set it in a slotted spoon or flatten it down into a colander and see what happens.

Observations What happens to the quicksand when you squeeze it? What happens when you let it go?

Now Try This! Experiment with adding more or less cornstarch to the mixture. How does it change the quicksand's behavior?

The Hows and Whys Cornstarch quicksand is a cool example of a non-Newtonian fluid because it gets more viscous when a force is applied and less viscous when that force is removed. In contrast, Newtonian fluids, like honey, become less viscous when the honey is warm and more viscous when the honey is cold.

CD HOVERCRAFT

LEVEL OF DIFFICULTY: MEDIUM
FROM BEGINNING TO END: 30 MINUTES
OTHER CATEGORIES: ENGINEERING

? How does a hovercraft work? How does it seamlessly glide over rough terrain? Construct a miniature version with a few household supplies to learn how a real hovercraft works.

MATERIALS

- CD or DVD
- Pop-top cap from a water bottle or dish soap bottle
- Duct tape
- Party balloon

THE STEPS

1. Start by sliding a CD or DVD across a hard tabletop or floor. How far does it slide before coming to a stop?

2. Now construct a hovercraft by attaching a pop-top cap over the center hole in the disc and taping the sides down with duct tape so there are no gaps and it is airtight.

3. Push the pop-top cap down to close it.

4. Inflate a balloon and then twist the end to keep the air from coming out.

5. Carefully stretch the mouth of the balloon over the pop-top cap and adjust the balloon so that it stands up directly over the center of the disc.

6. Place the hovercraft on a smooth surface and pop open the cap. Give it a small tap and watch what happens!

Observations How does the motion of the hovercraft compare with the motion of a plain disc? How far can each one slide across a surface before coming to a stop?

Now Try This! Can you add to the CD hovercraft to improve it? Experiment by building with supplies from the recycle bin to see if you can make the hovercraft glide higher or longer.

The Hows and Whys The airflow from the deflating balloon provides a pocket of resistance-free space on which the CD hovercraft can glide without encountering any friction. The air pushes down onto the surface, which lifts the disc just a little bit and allows it to freely hover. While our little CD hovercraft can only glide a few feet over a smooth surface, large-scale hovercraft are capable of gliding over all kinds of terrain, including rough land, snow, and water.

CRYSTAL GARDEN

LEVEL OF DIFFICULTY: MEDIUM
FROM BEGINNING TO END: 12 HOURS

? There are numerous examples of crystals that exist in nature, such as diamonds, pyrite, amethyst, and quartz. Have you ever wondered how crystals grow? Find out by growing your own salt crystal garden.

MATERIALS
- Epsom salt
- Clear glass jar
- Hot tap water
- Small pom-pom
- Measuring cups

THE STEPS

1. Measure 1 cup of Epsom salt and place it in the jar.

2. Measure 1 cup of very hot tap water and add it to the salt.

3. Stir the mixture well. It's fine if there is undissolved salt at the bottom of the jar.

4. Throw in the pom-pom and stir it up.

5. Place the jar in the refrigerator where it won't be disturbed and leave it overnight.

6. In the morning, check to see if the crystals grew. Carefully pour off the excess liquid from the jar to examine the crystals more closely.

7. It's okay to touch the crystals. Just be aware that they are delicate and may crumble.

Observations What do the crystals look like? What does the pom-pom look like?

Now Try This! Try growing crystals with other kinds of household materials to see how the crystals are similar or different. Some ideas to try include baking soda, table salt, sugar, or borax. (You may need to leave the jar in the refrigerator for a longer period for other crystals to form.)

The Hows and Whys More salt dissolves in hot water than in cooler water, creating an unstable supersaturated solution. As the solution cools down, the salt molecules come out of solution and crystallize easily onto any surface they stick to. The pom-pom is in the solution to provide nucleation sites, or uneven surfaces on which the crystals can easily start to grow.

DOES IT RUST?

? Why do some items rust and others don't? What causes rust? Answer all of these questions in this fun scientific inquiry.

MATERIALS

- Small paper cups
- Water
- Various metal objects from around the house, like nails, tacks, safety pins, paper clips, bobby pins, coins, and staples

THE STEPS

1. Fill each cup about halfway with water.

2. Drop one metal object into each cup.

3. Check on the cups each day for 7 days and record what you observe.

Observations Which objects got rusty? Were there any surprises?

Now Try This! Repeat this experiment with 2 of every metal object: Place one of them into filtered water and the other into water mixed with salt. Is there a difference in how fast oxidation occurs in salt water versus fresh water?

> **The Hows and Whys** Rust is a reddish brown substance called iron oxide that forms when iron metal comes into contact with oxygen. This chemical reaction is called oxidation. Since there is oxygen in water, it facilitates the rusting process.

EXPLODING BAGGIE

LEVEL OF DIFFICULTY: EASY

FROM BEGINNING TO END: 15 MINUTES

 You might be familiar with making a volcano out of baking soda and vinegar, but what happens if you put these 2 materials into a sealed plastic baggie? Learn about the chemical reaction between baking soda and vinegar while watching the pressure increase. The excitement will make you explode!

Caution: *Be sure to stay a few feet away from the baggie after adding the baking soda and closing the zip-top.*

MATERIALS

- Plastic zip-top baggie
- Vinegar
- Toilet paper
- Baking soda
- Measuring cups and spoons

THE STEPS

1. Be sure to conduct this experiment outside or somewhere else where it's okay if you make a little mess.

2. Measure and pour ½ cup vinegar into the baggie and set it aside.

3. Place 1 tablespoon baking soda on a couple squares of toilet paper. Fold and twist the tissue into a little pouch around the baking soda.

4. Quickly drop the baking soda pouch into the baggie and zip up the top of the baggie.

5. Give the baggie a few shakes, drop it on the ground, and take a few steps back.

Observations What happened to the baggie? What did you notice as baking soda and vinegar reacted together?

Now Try This! Change the variables to see how you can get the best pop from the baggie. Vary the amounts of baking soda and vinegar and the size of the baggie.

The Hows and Whys When baking soda and vinegar are mixed, they react to produce carbon dioxide gas. As more and more carbon dioxide fills up the baggie, the pressure inside increases. Once the pressure is so high that the baggie can't contain it any longer, the baggie pops!

FIREPROOF BALLOON

LEVEL OF DIFFICULTY: EASY
FROM BEGINNING TO END: 20 MINUTES
OTHER CATEGORIES: MATH

 What happens when you hold a balloon over a small flame? Learn about the conductive property of water and perform a surprising science trick using only a balloon and a candle.

Caution: *Always use caution around flames and matches. Ask an adult to help with this experiment.*

MATERIALS

- 2 party balloons
- Match
- Small candle
- Cold water

THE STEPS

1. Blow up a balloon and tie it off the end.

2. Use a match to light a small candle. Hold the balloon over the flame and watch what happens.

3. Fill up another balloon with a few ounces of cold water and then blow it up and tie it off.

4. Hold the water-filled balloon over the candle and slowly lower it over the flame.

Observations What happened to the second balloon? What was the difference?

Now Try This! Use a thermometer to measure the temperature of the water when you put it into the balloon. After doing this experiment, pop the balloon over a cup to capture the water so you can measure the temperature again. How many degrees did the temperature rise?

The Hows and Whys Water is able to absorb heat from the flame to keep the balloon cool. This prevents the balloon from popping, at least until the water gets warm enough that it is unable to continue to conduct heat away from the balloon.

FISHING FOR ICE

? If you live in a snowy place in the winter, you may have noticed that people often sprinkle salt on the ice on their steps, porches, and driveways. Do you know what happens to ice when it is mixed with salt? Find out by going fishing for ice with a string. You never know what you'll catch!

MATERIALS

- Cup of water
- Ice cubes
- String or yarn
- Table salt

THE STEPS

1. Place a few ice cubes into a cup of water.

2. Lay the string over the top of the ice cubes, trying to get it to touch each one.

3. Sprinkle some salt onto the top of the ice cubes and string.

4. Wait 1 minute. Gently pull the string out of the cup and see what you've caught!

Observations How many ice cubes can you freeze to the string at once?

Now Try This! What happens if you use other kinds of salt to go fishing for ice? Some ideas include Epsom salt, baking soda, and rock salt.

The Hows and Whys When salt is added to ice water, it decreases the freezing point. Pure water freezes at 32 degrees Fahrenheit, but the addition of salt decreases the freezing point by several degrees because salt molecules get in the way of water molecules freezing together. This means that the salt makes the ice melt. You can see how the salt melts little tunnels into the ice cubes.

However, since we are using only a tiny bit of salt in this experiment, the water around the ice quickly freezes again, freezing the string to the ice along with it. For a few moments, the ice sticks to the string.

FIRE EXTINGUISHER

LEVEL OF DIFFICULTY: MEDIUM
FROM BEGINNING TO END: 15 MINUTES

 How do fire extinguishers work to put out fires? Develop your own small-scale fire extinguisher to put out a small flame using a few ingredients you probably already have in the kitchen. Learn a new way to use a classic chemical reaction, too.

Caution: *Always be careful around matches and an open flame. Ask an adult to help with this experiment.*

MATERIALS

- Pint-size cup, jar, or bottle
- Measuring spoons
- 5 tablespoons vinegar
- Match
- Small candle or tea light
- ½ tablespoon baking soda

THE STEPS

1. Add the vinegar to a cup.

2. Use a match to light a small candle.

3. Add the baking soda to the vinegar.

4. Quickly, yet carefully, hold the cup at an angle over the candle to extinguish the flame (without pouring the vinegar mixture out of the cup).

Observations What made the flame go out? Why do you think a small flame goes out when you blow on it?

Now Try This! Vary the amounts of baking soda and vinegar to see how the reaction changes.

The Hows and Whys A flame requires oxygen to keep itself burning. If the oxygen is cut off or replaced with something else, the flame will quickly go out. In this chemical reaction, baking soda and vinegar mix to produce carbon dioxide gas. This is what you see bubbling up through the mixture. Carbon dioxide is heavier than air and drops right down onto the flame. This displaces the oxygen and extinguishes the flame as it flows out of the cup. Many fire extinguishers contain carbon dioxide, among other chemicals, to put out larger fires.

FLUFFY SOAP

LEVEL OF DIFFICULTY: EASY
FROM BEGINNING TO END: 20 MINUTES
OTHER CATEGORIES: MATH

Does a bar of soap sink or float? What happens when you cook soap in the microwave? Does all soap behave the same way? Discover the properties of bar soap and compare how various brands differ in this simple and surprising science experiment.

Caution: The soap will be hot when it comes out of the microwave, so be careful not to touch it right away. If at any point you smell something burning in the microwave, turn it off immediately.

MATERIALS

- Bowl of water
- Bar of Ivory soap
- Several bars of soap of other brands (like Irish Spring, Lever 2000, Olay, Dial, or others)
- Microwave-safe plate

THE STEPS

1. Place the bar of Ivory soap into the bowl of water to see if it sinks or floats. Record your observations.

2. Test out the other bars of soap one by one to discover if they sink or float.

3. Place the bar of Ivory soap on a microwave-safe dish. Cook it in the microwave for 1 minute, watching it through the door of the microwave. What happens?

4. Place the other bars of soap one by one in the microwave for 1 minute. (Remember: If you smell any burning soap, turn off the microwave immediately.) Record your observations of each brand.

Observations Is there a relationship between the density of a bar of soap and how it behaves when it is cooked in the microwave?

Now Try This! Weigh the bar of soap before and after it is cooked in the microwave. Does the weight change? Why?

The Hows and Whys Ivory soap is made by whipping a whole bunch of air into the mixture. Little air pockets get trapped in the soap, making it light and fluffy. The air pockets make the soap less dense than water, so the soap floats.

When Ivory soap is cooked in the microwave, it expands like a soap soufflé. This happens because water molecules stuck in the air pockets heat up and turn into water vapor. The water vapor escapes from the soap mixture, making it puff up and expand as it goes.

Other brands of soap have varying degrees of air whipped into them. How are they similar to/different from Ivory brand soap?

FOAM EXPLOSION

LEVEL OF DIFFICULTY: EASY

FROM BEGINNING TO END: 15 MINUTES

 Why does hydrogen peroxide come in a brown bottle? Take advantage of the tendency of hydrogen peroxide to decompose and learn how a catalyst works by making a really cool foam explosion.

Caution: *Hydrogen peroxide can irritate skin and bleach clothes. Use care when handling it.*

MATERIALS

- Glass or plastic 16-ounce bottle
- Liquid dish soap
- Measuring cups and spoons
- Food coloring
- ½ cup of 20 volume (6%) hydrogen peroxide (purchased from a beauty supply store or online)
- Baking dish or baking sheet
- Small plastic zip-top baggie
- 1 teaspoon dry yeast
- 2 tablespoons cool water
- Funnel

THE STEPS

1. Add a squirt of dish soap, a squirt of food coloring, and the hydrogen peroxide to a bottle. Mix well.

2. Place the bottle in a baking dish or on a baking sheet to catch the overflow.

3. Add the yeast and water to the baggie. Mix it up.

4. Use a funnel to pour the yeast mixture into the peroxide mixture. Do this step quickly because the reaction happens immediately!

5. The foamy mixture that explodes from the bottle is just soapy colored water. It is completely fine to touch, though the bottle will be a little bit warm because this is an exothermic reaction.

Observations Describe what happened when the yeast mixture was added to the peroxide solution. Were you surprised?

Now Try This! Try this chemical reaction again by varying the amount of yeast you add to the mixture. Is more or less foam produced depending on how much yeast is added?

The Hows and Whys Hydrogen peroxide naturally breaks down into water and oxygen gas. In this experiment, the yeast mixture acts as a catalyst, making this natural reaction happen more quickly. The oxygen gas bubbles out of the bottle so quickly it takes the soapy water with it, making it spill everywhere.

Most of the time, hydrogen peroxide comes in a brown plastic bottle to protect it from light exposure, which makes it break down quickly. (But not as quickly or as explosively as yeast does!)

FRUIT BOATS

LEVEL OF DIFFICULTY: EASY

FROM BEGINNING TO END: 20 MINUTES

 Which fruits can be made into boats that float? Does it matter if they have a peel? Make your own fruit boats and see if any of the results surprise you.

Caution: *Ask an adult for help cutting the fruit.*

MATERIALS

- An assortment of different fruits that you want to experiment with, like apples, oranges, kiwi fruit, bananas, pears, strawberries, grapefruit, and melons
- Knife
- Toothpicks
- Small triangular pieces of paper
- Large bowl of water

THE STEPS

1. Slice each piece of fruit in half. Peel the skin off one half and leave it on the other half.

2. Poke a toothpick through each piece of paper to make a little sail. Make enough sails for each piece of fruit.

3. Poke a sail into the cut side of each piece of fruit, but be sure not to pierce the skin on the unpeeled halves.

4. Place each piece of fruit into the water to see if it sinks or floats.

Observations Which pieces of fruit sink? Which ones float? Does it make a difference if the peel is on or off? Did any of the results surprise you?

Now Try This! Slice up the fruit into smaller pieces. Does slicing them up change their density?

The Hows and Whys Some fruit, such as apples, contain a lot of tiny air pockets. This makes them less dense than water, meaning they float. They make great boats!

Other fruits, such as oranges, are more dense than water when they are peeled. However, the peel contains many air pockets, including air that is trapped between the peel and the fruit. These fruits float with the peel on, but they sink without the peel. And, of course, some fruits just sink with or without the peel because they are more dense than water.

UNLEAKABLE BAGGIE

LEVEL OF DIFFICULTY: EASY

FROM BEGINNING TO END: 15 MINUTES

? If you poke sharp pencils through a baggie full of water, what do you think will happen? Find out by trying it yourself, preferably over the head of an adult! In this fun and easy science experiment, you will learn about polymers and see them in action.

MATERIALS

- Plastic zip-top baggie
- Water
- Several sharpened pencils

THE STEPS

1. Fill up the baggie about ¾ of the way with water. Squeeze out the air and make sure the top is zipped up tight.

2. Hold the baggie in one hand and use your other hand to stab a sharp pencil all the way through the baggie and out the other side.

3. Continue to impale the baggie with as many pencils as you have.

Observations Did any water spill?

Now Try This! What happens if you try this experiment using a plastic grocery bag? How about a water balloon?

The Hows and Whys Plastic storage bags are made of a polymer called low-density polyethylene. When the pencil pierces the plastic, the sharp end of the pencil squeezes through the chains of the polymer without breaking them. These chains are very flexible and actually move over to form a seal around the edge of the pencil so that no water is spilled from the baggie.

HEAVY AS A PIECE OF PAPER

LEVEL OF DIFFICULTY: EASY
FROM BEGINNING TO END: 5 MINUTES

? Which do you think will fall faster to the ground: a piece of paper or a large rock? Head outside on a balcony or to the top of a play structure to find out.

MATERIALS
- Piece of paper
- Large rock

THE STEPS

1. Hold the piece of paper in one hand and the rock in the other. Which is heavier? Which will fall to the ground faster?

2. Crumple up the piece of paper into the smallest, tightest ball you can.

3. Stand somewhere that you can safely drop a rock to the ground without hitting anyone or anything.

4. Drop the rock and the piece of paper at the same time from the same height.

Observations Which item landed first?

Now Try This! Take 2 pieces of paper of identical weight. Crumple one up and leave the other one flat. Drop them from the same height at the same time. Which one landed first? Why?

The Hows and Whys All objects are pulled toward the Earth by gravity. The acceleration of an object due to gravity is the same on everything, regardless of the object's weight. This means that you could drop a piano and a marble from the same height at the same time and they would land on the ground at exactly the same moment.

HOW DO ARCTIC ANIMALS STAY WARM?

LEVEL OF DIFFICULTY: EASY
FROM BEGINNING TO END: 20 MINUTES
OTHER CATEGORIES: MATH

? Have you ever wondered how Arctic animals stay warm in the most frigid, freezing conditions on Earth? Head to the kitchen and pretend to be a walrus or a polar bear to find out.

MATERIALS

- Bowl full of ice water
- Shortening

THE STEPS

1. Place a bare finger in the bowl of ice water. Count how many seconds you can stand to leave it there before it gets too cold.

2. Pull your finger out and warm it up.

3. Get some help to coat one finger with a thick layer of shortening. Be sure that no skin is visible.

4. Place the shortening-covered finger in the ice water and measure how long you can leave it there now.

Observations Could you feel the cold water through the layer of shortening? How long did you leave your finger in the ice water?

Now Try This! Try coating a finger with other substances to see if it insulates like shortening does. Be sure to measure how long you can leave your finger in the ice water each time and keep track of the results. Some ideas to try include peanut butter, butter, a piece of bread, and whipped cream.

The Hows and Whys Shortening is made of fat. In this experiment, it simulates the layer of blubber that Arctic animals, like seals, whales, walruses, and polar bears, have on their bodies to insulate them from the cold. It makes a huge difference, doesn't it?

NAKED EGG

LEVEL OF DIFFICULTY: EASY
FROM BEGINNING TO END: 24 HOURS

? What happens to an egg when it is soaked in vinegar? In this experiment, you will learn about the reaction between an acid and a base, plus you'll get to create something you've probably never seen before.

 Caution: *Always wash your hands with soap and water after you handle raw eggs.*

MATERIALS

- 3 cups or jars
- White vinegar
- Food coloring
- 3 whole eggs

THE STEPS

1. Fill the cups or jars with enough vinegar to cover an egg.

2. Add a few drops of food coloring to each cup of vinegar and mix them in.

3. Carefully add an egg to each cup.

4. Place the cups in the refrigerator and leave them overnight. Check on them every few hours to see how they are changing.

Observations What did you notice about the eggs as they soaked in vinegar? What do they look like after 24 hours? What do they feel like?

Now Try This! Fill up 3 new cups with different clear liquids. Some ideas to try include corn syrup, honey, hand soap, soda, salt water, and soapy water. Place an egg into a different liquid each night in the refrigerator and see what happens.

The Hows and Whys The eggshell dissolves because vinegar is an acid and the eggshell is made of a base called calcium carbonate. The vinegar breaks apart the solid calcium carbonate crystals that make up the eggshell into their calcium and carbonate parts. The calcium floats free, while the carbonate reacts to make carbon dioxide (these are the tiny air bubbles on the surface of the eggshell).

ICE CREAM IN A BAG

LEVEL OF DIFFICULTY: EASY
FROM BEGINNING TO END: 30 MINUTES
OTHER CATEGORIES: MATH

? What happens when salt is added to ice? How does the temperature change? Find out and measure the change for yourself, plus get rewarded with a delicious frosty treat for all your hard work.

MATERIALS

- 2 large mixing bowls
- Measuring cups and spoons
- 20 cups ice (divided)
- 2 cups water (divided)
- 6 tablespoons salt
- Thermometer
- Small plastic zip-top baggie
- ½ cup milk
- 1 tablespoon sugar
- ¼ teaspoon vanilla
- Gallon-size plastic zip-top baggie
- Spoon

THE STEPS

1. In one mixing bowl, mix 10 cups of ice and 1 cup of water.

2. In the other mixing bowl, mix 10 cups of ice, 1 cup of water, and the salt.

3. Wait a few minutes, then use a thermometer to measure the temperature of each bowl. Which mixture is colder?

4. Add the milk, sugar, and vanilla to the small baggie. Squeeze the air out and seal it up tightly.

5. Dump the salty ice mixture from the second bowl into the large baggie.

6. Place the small baggie inside the large baggie with the ice mixture and seal it.

7. Shake up the baggies for 5 to 10 minutes, or until the milk mixture turns into a soft solid.

8. Open up the large baggie and remove the small baggie. Rinse it under cold water, paying special attention to rinse off the zippered top of the baggie.

9. Open the bag, grab a spoon, and enjoy your sweet treat!

Observations What is the temperature of the salty ice mixture? How does the milk mixture freeze into ice cream so quickly?

Now Try This! Instead of mixing up the small baggie in the salty ice mixture, try placing it directly in the freezer. How is it the same? How is it different?

The Hows and Whys To make any variety of homemade ice cream, milk needs to be partially frozen. Most freezers are set at –10 degrees Fahrenheit, so putting milk directly in the freezer and leaving it there makes the milk freeze solid, which makes the texture chunky and icy instead of smooth and creamy. Water freezes at 32 degrees Fahrenheit, but because milk contains proteins and fat, it freezes at a lower temperature. This means that trying to freeze milk with ice cubes won't work. When salt is added to ice, it lowers the freezing point of the ice, making it melt. This leaves a salty ice mixture that is much colder than 32 degrees Fahrenheit. The temperature of the salty mixture is close to 0 degrees Fahrenheit! (You can verify this with a thermometer.) This temperature is cold enough to freeze milk into homemade ice cream in less than 10 minutes without freezing it solid.

LAVA LAMP

LEVEL OF DIFFICULTY: EASY

FROM BEGINNING TO END: 15 MINUTES

What happens when you add Alka-Seltzer tablets to a cup of water? What if you add a layer of oil over the top? In this experiment, you will make your own lava lamp, learn about acids and bases, experiment with density, and have a ton of fun.

MATERIALS

- Clear jar or cup
- Water
- Food coloring
- Vegetable oil
- Alka-Seltzer tablets
- Measuring cups

THE STEPS

1. Measure 1 cup of water into a jar.

2. Add a few drops of food coloring to the water and stir it around.

3. Measure 1 cup of vegetable oil into the jar. Where does the oil settle?

4. Break up an Alka-Seltzer tablet into fourths. Drop one fourth into the water-and-oil mixture and watch what happens.

5. Continue adding Alka-Seltzer tablets, and enjoy your lava lamp!

CONTINUED ➡

Observations Why don't oil and water mix? Why does oil settle on the top with the water on the bottom?

Now Try This! Make a lava lamp out of different kinds of oils and different kinds of clear liquids to see how it changes. Some oils to try include olive oil and mineral oil. Other clear liquids to use instead of water include rubbing alcohol and soda.

The Hows and Whys Alka-Seltzer tablets are made of sodium bicarbonate (a base) and dry citric acid (an acid). When a tablet is placed in water, these 2 substances mix and react just like baking soda and vinegar. They produce carbon dioxide gas, which is what you see bubbling up through the lava lamp. The bubbles take a little bit of water with them up through the oil layer, but because oil and water don't mix, the water droplets fall back down. This creates a delightful bubbly dance between the water and oil.

RIGHT OR LEFT?

? What happens to light when it passes through a cup full of water? Learn about the behavior of light and refraction by experimenting with this cool science trick.

MATERIALS

- Piece of paper
- Marker
- Tape
- Tall clear jar or cup
- Water

THE STEPS

1. Use a marker to draw a horizontal arrow on the piece of paper.

2. Tape the paper to the wall, or prop it up against some books so that it stands up by itself.

3. Place a jar in front of the paper so that you can see the arrow through it.

4. While watching the arrow through the cup, slowly pour water into it. Be sure to pour the water higher than the level of the arrow.

Observations What appeared to happen to the arrow as the water in the cup covered it?

Now Try This! Move the cup around and watch how the shape and position of the arrow changes. Does it change if the cup is closer to or farther away from the paper? What if you use a square glass rather than a round one? Can you make an estimation of where the focal point is?

The Hows and Whys When light passes through the cup, it gets refracted, or bent and focused toward the center into a focal point on the other side. After light passes through the focal point, the light that was on the left comes out on the right and vice versa. This makes the image appear to reverse.

SCATTERED PEPPER

LEVEL OF DIFFICULTY: EASY
FROM BEGINNING TO END: 10 MINUTES

? What happens when dish soap is dripped into water? Why? Create the illusion that pepper is fleeing from a drop of soap in this fun and easy science experiment.

MATERIALS

- Baking dish, baking pan, deep plate, or wide bowl that is at least ½ inch deep
- Water
- Black pepper
- Liquid dish soap

THE STEPS

1. Pour enough water into a dish so that it is about ½ inch deep.

2. Sprinkle pepper onto the water.

3. Squeeze a drop of liquid dish soap into the center of the plate.

Observations What happens when dish soap is dripped into the water?

Now Try This! Repeat this experiment using salt water instead of tap water. How are the results the same or different?

The Hows and Whys The molecules on the surface of a liquid bond tightly together to form a little dome. This is called surface tension. Pepper is light enough to float on water's surface without breaking the surface tension. However, when soap is dripped into the water, all the soap molecules bond with water molecules, which breaks the surface tension. The dome pops and all the surface water molecules spread out, taking the pepper with them.

SINK OR FLOAT?

? Does an egg sink or float? Perhaps the answer depends on the liquid the egg is in! You may be surprised by the results.

MATERIALS

- 6 cups
- Cold water
- Vegetable oil
- Measuring cups and spoons
- 3 tablespoons salt
- 3 tablespoons baking soda
- 3 tablespoons cornstarch
- 3 tablespoons flour
- 6 eggs

THE STEPS

1. Measure 1 cup of water into 5 of the cups. Measure 1 cup of oil into the last cup.

2. Leave one cup of plain water. This is the scientific control.

3. Add the salt to the second cup of water and stir.

4. Add the baking soda to the third cup and stir.

5. Add the cornstarch to the fourth cup and stir.

6. Add the flour to the fifth cup and stir.

7. Place 1 egg in each cup and observe what happens.

Observations In which liquids does the egg sink and in which ones does it float? Why?

Now Try This! Use hot water instead of cold. Keep adding solute until it no longer dissolves in the water to create a supersaturated solution. When you add an egg to each solution, do you get the same results as you did when using cold water?

The Hows and Whys An egg is more dense than water, so it sinks. However, when salt or other solutes are dissolved into the water, the solution becomes more dense. In some cases, the mixture is more dense than the egg, so the egg floats on top.

RAINBOW RAIN

? What happens when water is dripped into a cup full of oil? Create a beautiful rainbow rainstorm while learning about the interaction between oil and water.

MATERIALS

- Mineral oil
- Clear glass or plastic cup
- Several smaller cups
- Water
- Food coloring
- Plastic pipette or medicine dropper

THE STEPS

1. Pour about 1 cup of mineral oil into a clear cup and set it aside.

2. Fill several smaller cups with water. Add a few drops of food coloring to each one to create a variety of different-colored water.

3. Use a pipette to gently drip colored water into the clear cup of oil.

Observations What happened when water was added to oil?

Now Try This! Put a lid on the cup and shake up the oil and water mixture. What happens when everything settles back down?

The Hows and Whys Everything in our world is made of molecules that are held together by chemical bonds. Oil is made of nonpolar chemical bonds, while water is made of polar chemical bonds. These 2 kinds of bonds do not mix together, which is why oil and water do not mix.

Did you notice how the water settled on the bottom of the oil layer? This happens because water is more dense than oil.

SKY AND SUNSET JAR

LEVEL OF DIFFICULTY: EASY

FROM BEGINNING TO END: 10 MINUTES

? Why is the sky blue? Why does it look pink or orange during sunset and sunrise? Create your own sky in a jar and discover for yourself why the sky appears different colors at different times.

MATERIALS

- Clear glass jar or cup
- Milk
- Water
- Flashlight
- Measuring cups and spoons

THE STEPS

1. Measure 2 teaspoons of milk and add it to a jar.

2. Fill the jar with 2 cups of water and mix it with the milk to make a cloudy white mixture.

3. In a dark room, hold a flashlight to one side of the jar and shine it through the jar.

4. Next, move the flashlight so that it is behind the jar, pointing directly at you.

Observations What color is the mixture when the flashlight shines through the jar on the side? What about when it is behind the jar?

Now Try This! How does the color of the mixture change if you add more or less milk? How does this apply to the sky outside?

The Hows and Whys White light from the sun is made of all the colors of the rainbow. You can see this when sunlight passes through a prism. Each color travels through the air in waves of different sizes. Blue light has a shorter wavelength than red light, meaning that blue light travels in short, choppy waves and red light travels in long, lazy waves.

When sunlight enters Earth's atmosphere, it is scattered in many directions by gases in the air, such as oxygen and nitrogen. Because blue light has a short, high-frequency wavelength, it gets scattered the most. This causes the sky to appear blue when you look at it during the day.

Red light's wavelength is longer, with a lower frequency, so it gets scattered the least by atmospheric gas molecules. When the sun is lower in the horizon at sunrise or sunset, its light passes through more of the atmosphere to reach your eyes. Most of the blue light has been scattered out and away from the line of sight, leaving the reds, oranges, and yellows to pass straight through to your eyes.

SOUND WAVES EXPERIMENT

LEVEL OF DIFFICULTY: EASY
FROM BEGINNING TO END: 10 MINUTES

? Can you hear vibrations? Learn how sound travels by doing this really cool sound waves experiment and making your very own gong with a kitchen spoon.

MATERIALS
- Metal spoon
- 4 feet of string or yarn
- Ruler

THE STEPS

1. Tie the handle of the spoon to the middle of the string.

2. Wrap each end of the string a few times around your index fingers.

3. Hold your fingers up close to your ears and let the spoon hang free at your waist.

4. Have a friend hit the spoon with the ruler.

Observations What can you hear when your friend hits the spoon with the ruler? Does it sound different when the string is held close versus holding the string far away from your ears? How long does the sound echo?

Now Try This! Try attaching different sizes of spoons and forks to the string to see how they each sound when hit with a ruler.

The Hows and Whys Sound is simply vibrations that travel through the air or through another medium. In this experiment, hitting the spoon with a ruler makes the spoon vibrate. Those vibrations travel up through the string into your ears, which your brain interprets as sound.

SODA CAN SUBMARINE

LEVEL OF DIFFICULTY: EASY
FROM BEGINNING TO END: 15 MINUTES

? How does a submarine dive deep into the water and come up to the surface again? Experiment with your own submarine to find out.

MATERIALS

- Empty soda can
- 3 feet of vinyl tubing
- Water
- Tall vase or pitcher with an opening wide enough to fit the soda can

THE STEPS

1. Place one end of the tubing into the soda can.

2. Fill the soda can with water.

3. Fill a vase ¾ full of water.

4. Put one end of the tubing in the soda can and place the soda can in the vase. Use the tubing to stir up the water inside the soda can to work out any extra air bubbles.

5. If the soda can doesn't sink, get another small cup full of water and top off the water level in the soda can. In order for it to sink, there can't be any open space left for air bubbles.

6. Once the soda can sinks, blow into the tube. Keep this end of the tubing higher than the water level in the vase, so you don't get a mouthful of water when you're done blowing. Watch as air travels through the tube into the submarine, making it surface again!

Observations What do you notice when air is being blown into the tubing? What happens to the water in the vase?

Now Try This! Can you design and build a submarine using an empty tin can or a plastic bottle? Look through the recycle bin to see what materials you have available.

The Hows and Whys As air flows into the can, water is displaced and flows out. These air bubbles make the soda can less dense than the surrounding water, making it rise to the surface. Real submarines are designed to have ballast tanks. These tanks can be alternately filled with water or air, depending on whether the submarine needs to dive or surface.

WALKING ON EGGS

LEVEL OF DIFFICULTY: EASY

FROM BEGINNING TO END: 10 MINUTES

? Can you walk on raw eggs without cracking them? Test how strong eggs really are by standing on them and walking across them with bare feet.

! Caution: *This experiment can get a bit messy. Be sure to either put down a drop cloth underneath the egg cartons or do this experiment outside.*

MATERIALS

- Drop cloth
- 6 dozen eggs in cartons

THE STEPS

1. Open the egg cartons and lay them end to end in 2 rows so that there are 3 cartons in each row.

2. Take off your shoes and socks. Carefully step onto the first carton of eggs with one foot. You may need to use a friend or a chair for some support.

3. Step onto the second row of eggs with the other foot. Carefully walk across the eggs while keeping your feet as flat as possible.

CONTINUED ➡

Observations Did any of the eggs crack? Is there a technique that works best to walk across the eggs without breaking them?

Now Try This! Take one open carton of eggs and stack heavy books one at a time on top of them. How many books can the eggs support before they crack? Can you arrange the eggs in the carton differently to support more books?

The Hows and Whys Eggs are shaped similarly to a three-dimensional arch, one of the strongest architectural forms. Their curved shape distributes pressure evenly all over the shell and makes them very strong. However, they don't withstand uneven forces, which is why they crack easily against a bowl or break if you walk across them on your heels.

WHAT DISSOLVES IN WATER?

LEVEL OF DIFFICULTY: EASY
FROM BEGINNING TO END: 30 MINUTES

? Which substances dissolve in water? Which substances don't? Get out your mixing spoon, and discover the answer for yourself.

MATERIALS

- Several clear cups
- Water
- Several different substances to test, like salt, pepper, sugar, flour, sand, coffee, oatmeal, sprinkles, oil, cornmeal, Kool-Aid, and spices
- Mixing spoons
- Measuring spoons

THE STEPS

1. Measure an equal amount of water into each cup.

2. Add 1 teaspoon of one substance to one cup, another teaspoon of a different substance to another cup, and so on. Use mixing spoons to stir each solution.

3. Observe and record what happens in each cup. What color is the solution? Did the substance dissolve in water?

Observations Which items disappeared into the water when you stirred? Do you think that they are still there? How could you figure this out?

Now Try This! Use hot water to repeat this experiment with the same pantry items. Does the temperature of the water affect whether a substance dissolves in it?

The Hows and Whys Water molecules are made of polar bonds, meaning they each have a slightly positive end and a slightly negative end. Similar to the way magnets attract other magnets, the positive end of one polar molecule attracts the negative end of another polar molecule. When something like salt is added to water, the positive part of the water molecule attracts the negative part of the salt, while the negative part of the water molecule attracts the positive part of the salt. This is why water will dissolve anything else that is polar or carries a charge, like salt, but it won't dissolve something that is made of nonpolar bonds, like olive oil.

WALKING RAINBOW

LEVEL OF DIFFICULTY: EASY

FROM BEGINNING TO END: 12 HOURS

OTHER CATEGORIES: ART

? Have you ever wondered how gigantic trees get water from their roots all the way up to their highest leaves and branches? Making a walking water rainbow is an easy and colorful hands-on way to discover the answer to this question.

MATERIALS

- 6 pint-size Mason jars or clear cups
- Water
- Food coloring in each of the primary colors (red, yellow, and blue)
- Paper towels
- Measuring cups

THE STEPS

1. Add 2 cups of water and 20 drops of red food coloring to a jar. Add 2 cups of water and 20 drops of yellow food coloring to another jar. Add 2 cups of water and 20 drops of blue food coloring to a third jar.

2. Arrange the 6 jars in a circle so that there is an empty jar in between each full jar.

3. Tear off 6 paper towels. Fold each one a few times lengthwise so that it fits easily into the mouth of a jar.

4. Insert the paper towels so that one end touches the bottom of one full jar and the other end touches the bottom of an empty jar. You should have a circle where each jar has 2 paper towels coming into it.

5. Watch and observe what happens over the next few minutes and hours.

Observations How was a secondary color made in the empty jar?

Now Try This! Instead of leaving some jars empty, try filling all of the jars with 2 cups of water. Arrange them in the same circular pattern as above: blue, clear, red, clear, yellow, clear. What happens?

The Hows and Whys Paper towels are made from trees, which means they are made of plant fibers called cellulose. Water moves up through cellulose because of 2 forces: adhesion and cohesion. Adhesion is the attraction between water molecules and cellulose fibers, while cohesion is the attraction between 2 water molecules. Water molecules are attracted to the cellulose fibers, which makes them move through the fibers. However, water molecules are also attracted to one another and continue to pull one another up. Both of these forces working together makes a phenomenon occur called capillary action, meaning that water defies gravity and flows upward!

YEAST BALLOON

LEVEL OF DIFFICULTY: EASY
FROM BEGINNING TO END: 60 MINUTES

? Perhaps you are familiar with yeast, a key ingredient when making bread dough, pizza dough, or dinner rolls. But do you know how yeast works? Perform a little science magic trick by inflating a balloon without even blowing into it and learn all about how yeast works to make dough rise.

MATERIALS

- 2 tablespoons dried yeast
- 1 tablespoon sugar
- 2 tablespoons lukewarm water
- Clear 16-ounce bottle with a narrow neck
- Bowl full of lukewarm water
- Party balloon
- Measuring spoons

THE STEPS

1. Mix the yeast, sugar, and 2 tablespoons water in the bottle.

2. Place the bottle into the bowl of water to keep it warm.

3. Stretch a balloon over the mouth of the bottle. Check in every few minutes to observe what is happening.

Observations How does the yeast mixture change over time? What do you notice happening in the bottle?

Now Try This! Vary the amounts of sugar, yeast, and water you add to the bottle to see how big you can inflate the balloon.

The Hows and Whys Yeast is a tiny fungus that converts sugar into alcohol and carbon dioxide. To do this, it needs to be wet and warm. In this experiment, the balloon captures the carbon dioxide as the yeast produces it, causing the balloon to inflate on its own!

Yeast works the same way in dough, except the carbon dioxide bubbles get trapped in the dense dough. This makes the dough expand into light and fluffy bread.

Chapter Three

TECHNOLOGY

Prepare yourself to dive into the world of invisible forces that rule our technological world!

In this chapter, you will invent your own electrical circuits; use electrons to bend water; manipulate magnets; create lightning; and make your own batteries, electromagnets, telephones, and compasses.

Two of the main topics covered are electricity and magnetism. These two subjects form the foundation on which our current technology is based. You will also explore different sources of machine power, such as wind, hot air, and chemical reactions.

Technology is defined as the application of science to solve a problem. It is constantly evolving to become faster, cheaper, and more functional. The experiments in this chapter will give you a solid foundational education about the technological guts that power up devices we use every day. This will be a springboard into learning about current technology and developing inventions we haven't even imagined yet.

We all interface with technology daily. But do you know how it really works? Do you know why a lamp turns on when you click a switch? Do you know why the doorbell rings when a button is pushed? Do you know how a battery stores energy? You will find the answers to these questions, and more, by doing the experiments in this chapter.

You will need a few items, like magnets and simple electronic supplies, that can be easily and inexpensively found online or at an electronics store. Be sure to read over the materials list and gather what you need before diving into an experiment. For your convenience, here is a list of all the electronic and hardware supplies for the entire chapter:

- 5 alligator-clip wires
- 5mm LEDs (red and blue)
- AA battery holder with wires
- 3 feet insulated copper wire
- Copper tape, ¼ inch wide and double-sided conductive (available online for about $6 or in hardware stores as slug tape)
- 1 empty sewing bobbin
- 4 zinc-galvanized nails
- Iron nail (3 to 6 inches long)
- Wire stripper
- Bar magnet, with north and south clearly indicated

Have a wonderful time discovering the exciting world of technology, circuits, magnets, and batteries!

MAGIC SPOON

LEVEL OF DIFFICULTY: EASY
FROM BEGINNING TO END: 10 MINUTES
OTHER CATEGORIES: SCIENCE

? Is there a way you can separate pepper from a mixture of salt and pepper? In this science experiment, you will make a "magic" spoon and experiment with different ways to make it pick up ground pepper.

MATERIALS:

- Small bowl
- Salt
- Ground pepper
- Plastic spoon
- Dishcloth
- Measuring spoons

THE STEPS

1. Measure 1 teaspoon each of salt and pepper into a small bowl and mix them together.

2. Rub a plastic spoon on a dishcloth for about 10 seconds.

3. Hold the rounded end of the spoon over the salt and pepper mixture. What happens?

Observations Why do you think the pepper jumps and leaves the salt behind? Does the effect change if you alter the distance or the angle of the spoon relative to the salt and pepper?

Now Try This! Experiment with different ways to give the spoon a charge. Rub it in your hair, rub it with some wool, or rub it against your shirt to see if it changes how charged the spoon gets.

The Hows and Whys When the spoon is rubbed against the dishcloth, electrons are transferred between the 2 materials, causing a charge imbalance. This creates static electricity. When the spoon is charged, it can attract small objects, like ground pepper. You may notice that both salt and pepper are attracted to the spoon, but pepper is lighter, so it is attracted first and sticks longer.

CONDUCTIVITY EXPERIMENT

LEVEL OF DIFFICULTY: MEDIUM
FROM BEGINNING TO END: 45 MINUTES

? Do you know which items are good conductors of electricity? Learn about electrical circuits by building one of your own and then use it to test items around your house to see if they are conductive.

MATERIALS

- AA battery holder with wires
- 2 AA batteries
- 3 alligator-clip wires
- 5mm LED
- Various household objects (some metallic and some not metallic), such as safety pins, paper clips, bracelets, pencils, nails, screws, earrings, plastic toys, and coins

THE STEPS

1. Place the batteries in the battery holder.

2. Connect an alligator clip to each of the battery holder wires.

3. Double-check to make sure the circuit is working by connecting the other ends of the alligator-clip wires to the pins on the LED. If it lights up, the circuit is working. If it doesn't, swap the pins the alligator clips are attached to. If it still doesn't work, replace the batteries with fresh ones.

4. Once you know your circuit is working, disconnect one alligator clip from the LED pin.

5. Attach the third alligator-clip wire to the LED pin. You should have 2 free alligator clips.

6. Attach the 2 free alligator clips to each household item, one at a time. Make a hypothesis before hooking each object to the circuit about whether the light will turn on.

Observations Which objects enabled the light to turn on? Which ones didn't? Which objects are conductors?

Now Try This! Experiment with building more of your own circuits. Can you add another alligator-clip wire and LED to the circuit? Can you make a closed circuit with 2 metallic conductors right next to each other?

The Hows and Whys Electricity requires a complete loop for the current to flow. This is called a closed circuit. If the path is broken or blocked in any way, the current cannot flow and it becomes an open circuit. Metallic items, like pennies, will create a closed circuit because they allow electricity to flow through them, while items that are insulators (like plastic toys, which don't conduct electricity) will keep the circuit open.

FLYING BIRDS

LEVEL OF DIFFICULTY: EASY
FROM BEGINNING TO END: 20 MINUTES
OTHER CATEGORIES: SCIENCE

Can you make paper birds fly using a balloon? Use the power of static electricity to magically pick up paper and move it around.

MATERIALS

- Tissue paper
- Markers
- Scissors
- Party balloon
- Wool cloth

THE STEPS

1. Using markers, draw a few birds on tissue paper and cut them out with scissors.

2. Lay the paper birds on a flat surface.

3. Inflate a balloon and tie it off at the end.

4. Rub the balloon on wool cloth or on your hair for 10 to 20 seconds.

5. Hold the balloon a few inches above the paper birds. See if you can make them fly without touching them!

Observations What happens when the balloon gets close to the paper birds? What happens if you point the other side of the balloon toward the paper birds?

Now Try This! Draw more birds on heavier paper (like card stock) and try to pick them up with a statically charged balloon. Do they fly?

The Hows and Whys When a balloon is rubbed with wool cloth, electrons are transferred from the cloth to the balloon. This gives the balloon an overall negative charge. Even though the paper has a neutral charge, the charges within it can rearrange so that a positively charged area is attracted by the negatively charged balloon.

IRON FOR BREAKFAST

LEVEL OF DIFFICULTY: MEDIUM
FROM BEGINNING TO END: 45 MINUTES
OTHER CATEGORIES: SCIENCE

? Iron is a very important mineral that everyone needs to eat every day. Many breakfast cereals claim that they contain iron, but do they really? Pull out your magnet set and find out.

MATERIALS

- Iron-fortified cereal
- Quart-size plastic zip-top baggie
- Warm water
- Magnet (the strongest one you have available)
- Measuring cups

THE STEPS

1. Pour 1 cup of cereal into the baggie. Crush it up with your fingers through the plastic.

2. Fill the baggie up halfway with warm water. Seal the baggie securely, trapping an air pocket in the bag.

3. Shake up the mixture for about 1 minute and then let it sit for about 20 minutes while the cereal dissolves.

4. Hold your strongest magnet in your hand and place the bag of cereal soup on top of the magnet. Move the magnet around in slow circles, always keeping it in contact with the bag.

5. Carefully flip the bag and magnet over so that the magnet is now on top. Gently move the bag so that the magnet is right over the air pocket.

6. Continue moving the magnet in small circles to get the iron to clump together so that it is easier to see.

Observations What did you observe as the magnet moved around the cereal soup?

Now Try This! Is there a way you can get the iron filings out of the bag and weigh them on a kitchen scale? Test other kinds of breakfast cereal, rice cereal for babies, or other foods that are iron fortified to see how much iron you can extract from each one.

The Hows and Whys Since iron is a metal that is attracted to magnets, you can extract it from foods to which it has been added.

WIND-POWERED CAR

LEVEL OF DIFFICULTY: EASY
FROM BEGINNING TO END: 45 MINUTES
OTHER CATEGORIES: ENGINEERING, MATH

? Can you design and build a sail to attach to a toy car that will make the car move, powered only by the wind? Have a race with a friend to see whose car goes the farthest.

MATERIALS

- Craft supplies, such as paper, craft sticks, index cards, wooden skewers, plastic bags, and string
- Scissors
- Tape
- Toy car
- Fan or blow dryer
- Tape measure

THE STEPS

1. Construct a sail for a toy car using scissors and any craft supplies you have available at home.

2. Attach the sail to the car with tape.

3. Test out the sail by blowing air into it using a fan or a blow dryer. If you don't have access to either of these tools, you can just use your breath to blow into the sail.

4. Set up the wind-powered car directly in front of the source of the wind. Lay the tape measure out on the ground and tape it down so it doesn't get blown away.

5. Turn on the fan or blow dryer and see how far your car travels.

Observations What kinds of sail designs enable the toy car to travel the farthest? How can you modify your design to make it better?

Now Try This! Add a little bit of weight to the toy car by taping coins to it. How does this affect how far it travels?

The Hows and Whys Air is made up of particles, just like a liquid is. The faster the air moves, the faster those particles move. The sail captures the fast-moving air, pushing the car forward.

FLOATING COMPASS

LEVEL OF DIFFICULTY: EASY
FROM BEGINNING TO END: 10 MINUTES
OTHER CATEGORIES: SCIENCE

(?) Which way is the North Magnetic Pole? Use a magnet and a few household supplies to quickly and easily figure out exactly which direction is north.

MATERIALS
- Bar magnet, with north and south clearly indicated
- Tape
- Small plastic storage container with a flat bottom
- Large bowl full of water

THE STEPS

1. Tape the magnet inside the bottom of a small plastic storage container.

2. Place the plastic container into a large bowl full of water so that it floats.

3. Wait a few minutes for the small bowl to be still.

Observations Which way is north? Spin the small bowl and see if the magnet settles the same way.

Now Try This! Magnetize a needle by stroking the needle 20 times in the same direction with one end of the bar magnet. Cut out a small circle of paper and thread the needle through it, as you would a needle through cloth. Don't run the needle all the way through, but leave the needle halfway through the paper with the needle lying flat on the surface. Float the paper in a bowl full of water so that the ends of the needle are on top of the paper and see which direction the needle ends up pointing.

The Hows and Whys No matter how you move the small plastic container, it will always settle with the magnet pointing to the north. This is because Earth has a magnetic field that pulls on the bar magnet and aligns it facing north-south.

JET-POWERED SPEEDBOAT

LEVEL OF DIFFICULTY: EASY
FROM BEGINNING TO END: 20 MINUTES
OTHER CATEGORIES: SCIENCE, ENGINEERING

 Can you make a boat propel through the water on its own? Use a classic chemical reaction to provide the power and learn about Newton's third law of motion.

Caution: *This experiment can be very messy. Hold the boat over the bathtub as you secure the cap on.*

MATERIALS

- Plastic bottle with a pop-top cap
- Measuring cups and spoons
- Food coloring
- Toilet paper
- 1½ cups vinegar
- 1 tablespoon baking soda

(Note: You may need to double the amounts of baking soda and vinegar, depending on the size of the bottle.)

THE STEPS

1. Fill the bathtub with water until it is about 6 inches deep.

2. Make sure the bottle's pop-top cap is popped up, meaning it is open.

3. Unscrew the cap and add the vinegar to the bottle.

4. Add a few drops of food coloring.

5. Tear off 2 squares of toilet paper and lay them flat. Pour the baking soda on the squares and fold them up so that the baking soda is in a little pouch.

6. Hold the bottle over the bathtub. Drop the baking soda pouch into the vinegar in the bottle and quickly screw the cap on tight.

7. Let the bottle go in the water and watch your boat propel itself around.

Observations What happens to the boat after the cap is screwed on? What interesting things do you notice?

Now Try This! Experiment with different amounts of baking soda and vinegar to see how you can propel the boat even longer.

The Hows and Whys Newton's third law of motion states that for every action, there is an equal but opposite reaction. The action is the carbon dioxide bubbles rushing out the back of the boat and pushing against the water. The reaction is the water behind the boat pushing against the boat with the same force, causing the boat to move forward.

Baking soda and vinegar react to form carbon dioxide gas. As the carbon dioxide forcefully bubbles out, it takes some of the solution with it out the back.

BENDING WATER

LEVEL OF DIFFICULTY: EASY
FROM BEGINNING TO END: 10 MINUTES
OTHER CATEGORIES: SCIENCE

(?) Can you move running water from a faucet without touching it or adjusting the faucet? Use the power of static electricity to make water bend as if there were a string tied to it.

MATERIALS
- Water faucet
- Dry plastic comb

THE STEPS

1. Turn the water faucet on low so that a very slim stream of water flows from it.

2. Run the comb through your hair several times.

3. Hold the comb right next to, but not touching, the stream of water.

Observations What happens to the water when the comb gets close to it?

Now Try This! Does the temperature of the water affect how much it bends toward the comb? Can you try bending water with other objects, such as a statically charged balloon or a plastic spoon?

The Hows and Whys When you comb your hair, electrons gather onto the plastic comb. This builds up a static charge on the comb that attracts the stream of water, as if by magic. For this experiment to work, the air has to be somewhat dry. If it is too humid, the electrons that are built up on the comb cling to water molecules in the air instead. That means don't try to do this experiment in a steamy bathroom.

LEMON POWER!

LEVEL OF DIFFICULTY: MEDIUM
FROM BEGINNING TO END: 30 MINUTES
OTHER CATEGORIES: SCIENCE

 Can you turn on a light using fruit as the only power source? Give it a try and learn about circuits, electron flow, and how real batteries work.

Caution: *Ask an adult to help cut the lemon.*

MATERIALS:

- 4 lemons
- Knife
- 4 pennies
- 4 zinc-galvanized nails
- 5 alligator-clip wires
- 5mm LED

THE STEPS

1. Squeeze and roll the lemons to release the juice and pulp inside.

2. Use a kitchen knife to cut a small slit into each lemon.

3. Insert a penny halfway into each of the slits. Make sure the penny is touching the juicy insides of the lemon.

4. Push a nail into each lemon, being careful not to let it touch the penny.

5. Use 3 alligator clips to connect the penny from one lemon to the nail in a different lemon so that all 4 lemons are connected in a line.

6. Attach one end of another alligator clip to the last nail and the other end to the LED.

7. Attach the last alligator clip to the last penny and connect it to the LED.

8. The light should turn on! If it doesn't, disconnect the bulb, turn it around, and connect it again so that the 2 pins are attached to the opposite wires. Double-check to make sure the entire electric circuit is hooked up correctly.

CONTINUED ➡

Observations Why does the light turn on only if the entire circuit is hooked up correctly? Why does it work only in one direction?

Now Try This! Can you use other fruit to make a battery using the same equipment?

The Hows and Whys Batteries are made of 2 different kinds of metals that are suspended in an acidic solution. They are powered by the transfer of electrons from one metal to the other.

In a lemon battery, the 2 metals are zinc (from the galvanized nail) and copper (from the penny). Electrons are transferred from the nail to the penny through the acidic juices in the lemon. This creates a current that flows from each lemon into the LED, making it turn on.

MAGNET-POWERED CAR

LEVEL OF DIFFICULTY: EASY
FROM BEGINNING TO END: 10 MINUTES
OTHER CATEGORIES: SCIENCE

? Can you move a toy car around without ever touching it? You can, by turning a regular toy car into a magnet-powered car. Push it forward, make it turn, and park it using magnetism, an incredible invisible force.

MATERIALS
- Masking tape or painter's tape
- Toy car
- Bar magnet
- Magnetic wand or horseshoe magnet

THE STEPS

1. With an adult's permission, use masking tape or painter's tape to make a road on a smooth floor. Add parking lots and other highways on which to drive a toy car.

2. Tape a bar magnet securely to the top of the toy car.

3. Use a magnetic wand to push and pull the car around the floor. See if you can make the car turn around, go backward, and drive along the road without touching it with your hands.

Observations Did you find it easier to use your magnet to push or to pull the car along the road?

Now Try This! Make several magnet-powered cars and see how they interact as they drive into and next to one another.

The Hows and Whys Magnets have an invisible magnetic field around them that attracts other magnets and magnetic materials. One end of a magnet is the "north" end and the other end is the "south" end. Similar poles (north and north or south and south) repel each other, while poles that are different (north and south) attract each other. If you find that one end of the magnet repels something, flip it around to see if it will attract that same object. In this experiment, the magnetic force is strong enough to propel a toy car around the room.

PAPER CIRCUIT ART

LEVEL OF DIFFICULTY: MEDIUM
FROM BEGINNING TO END: 60 MINUTES
OTHER CATEGORIES: ART

? Electricity powers many devices we use every day. These devices all contain electrical circuits, or paths from which electrons flow. Can you create an artistic electrical circuit out of paper? Make a birthday card with candles that really light up or a picture of a constellation shining in the night sky using a few really cool electronic supplies.

! *Caution:* Coin cell batteries are *extremely dangerous if they are swallowed. Do not leave your card or any electronic supplies where a younger child can get them.*

MATERIALS

- Card stock
- Copper tape, ¼ inch wide and double-sided conductive (available online for about $6 or in hardware stores as slug tape)
- Scissors
- 3V coin cell battery
- 5mm LEDs
- Clear tape

THE STEPS

1. Make a simple paper circuit: Place copper tape on the card stock in the shape of a square, leaving a tiny gap in one of the sides of the square, using scissors as needed. Make sure 3 of the corners of the square are connected, but leave another space between the ends of the tape in the fourth corner.

2. At the open corner, place the bottom (negative side) of a coin cell battery on one end of the copper tape.

3. Using another piece of copper tape or a paperclip, connect the top (positive side) of the coin cell battery to the other end of the tape in the corner.

CONTINUED ➧

4. Place an LED in the gap you left in the side of the square, making sure both pins of the LED touch the tape.

5. If the LED turns on, you have it in the right place. You have just made a closed circuit! Secure it with clear tape.

6. If the LED does not turn on, flip it 180 degrees. LEDs work only in one direction.

7. Once you have succeeded at making a simple paper circuit, use your imagination to create a card for a friend using a circuit and LEDs.

Observations Why do you have to leave a gap for the LED to bridge? Will the light turn on without a gap in the tape?

Now Try This! Can you create a paper circuit card with an on/off switch? Hint: A paperclip attached to a metal brad (also called a paper fastener) rotates on paper very easily.

The Hows and Whys Electrons flow from the negative end of the battery around the entire closed electrical circuit through the copper tape. When the circuit is closed, the LED turns on. If it is left open, the LED will not turn on.

PENNY FLASHLIGHT

LEVEL OF DIFFICULTY: MEDIUM
FROM BEGINNING TO END: 45 MINUTES
OTHER CATEGORIES: ENGINEERING

Can you turn on a light with pennies? In this experiment, you will do just that by making your own flashlight out of stuff you have around the house.

MATERIALS

- Large cup filled with a small amount (about ½ cup) of water
- Salt
- Vinegar
- Scissors
- Cardboard
- 5 pennies dated after 1982
- Sandpaper
- Paper towel
- 5mm red LED
- Electrical tape
- Measuring spoons

THE STEPS

1. Make a supersaturated saltwater solution by adding salt to the cup of water until it won't dissolve anymore. You'll have some undissolved salt at the bottom of the cup.

2. Add 1 teaspoon of vinegar to the salt water.

3. Use scissors to cut four ½-inch squares of cardboard. Place these in the saltwater solution.

4. While the cardboard is soaking, use sandpaper on the "tails" side of 4 pennies to sand the copper completely off the surface. It works best to lay the sandpaper on a table and rub a penny back and forth until all the copper is gone. You should expose the shiny zinc core of the pennies.

5. Leave the fifth penny intact.

6. Remove the cardboard from the salt water and let the pieces dry on a paper towel for a few minutes.

CONTINUED →

7. Assemble the penny battery: Place one penny, copper-side down, on the bottom. Place a piece of wet cardboard on top of it. Add another penny, copper-side down, and another piece of cardboard. Continue the pattern so you end up with 4 layers of copper, zinc, and cardboard.

8. Place the fifth, intact penny on top.

9. Connect the LED by placing the longer pin on the top and the shorter pin on the bottom of the stack. If the light doesn't turn on, make sure that the pins are touching only the top and bottom surfaces of the stack, that none of the pennies are touching other pennies, and that none of the cardboard is touching other cardboard. Wipe excess salt water from the battery and try again.

10. Once the LED turns on, use electrical tape to wrap the battery together so it stays on. Now you have a homemade flashlight!

Observations Did the light turn on the first time you tried? Why or why not?

Now Try This! In this experiment, you made a battery with 4 cells. Can you make a battery with 5 or 6 cells that can turn on a blue LED, which requires a higher voltage than a red one? If you have a voltmeter, measure how much electricity is generated per cell.

The Hows and Whys Batteries are devices that convert chemical energy into electrical energy. They are powered by the transfer of electrons from one metal to another through an acidic solution. In this experiment, the acidic solution is salt water with vinegar. The 2 metals are copper on one side of the penny and zinc on the other side. As electrons are transferred from the zinc side of one penny to the copper side of the next penny, an electric current is created that is strong enough to light up a red LED.

MAGNETIC PUPPETS

LEVEL OF DIFFICULTY: EASY
FROM BEGINNING TO END: 30 MINUTES
OTHER CATEGORIES: SCIENCE, ENGINEERING

? Can you make a paper puppet fly using the power of magnetism? Do magnets attract objects through cardboard? Make your own cardboard box theater and experiment with magnetism to put on your own magnetic puppet show.

MATERIALS

- Cardboard box
- String
- Scissors
- Markers
- Paper
- Paperclip
- Tape
- Magnet

THE STEPS

1. Lay a cardboard box on its side with the open end facing you. Using scissors, cut a piece of string about the same length as the height of the box.

2. Use markers to draw a flying animal or machine, like a butterfly, a bird, a bat, an airplane, or a balloon, on a piece of paper and cut it out.

3. Tie one end of the string to the paperclip. Tape the paperclip to the back of the paper puppet.

4. Hold the puppet inside the box, almost touching the top. Pull the string down tight and tape the free end to the bottom of the box.

5. Lay a magnet on top of the box. Hold the paper puppet up near the magnet.

6. Try moving the magnet around the top of the box and watch what happens!

Observations What happens to the paper puppet when you move the magnet around?

Now Try This! Experiment with different magnets to see which ones work the best. Are some magnets stronger than others?

The Hows and Whys Metal paperclips are made from steel, which contains iron. The attraction between the magnet and the iron is strong enough for the magnet to pull on the paperclip, even through a cardboard box.

MAGNETIC PENDULUM

LEVEL OF DIFFICULTY: EASY

FROM BEGINNING TO END: 30 MINUTES

OTHER CATEGORIES: SCIENCE, ENGINEERING

? Can you make a magnetic pendulum that continues to swing and spin for several minutes? Arrange magnets on the floor, tie a magnet to a pivot point, and see which direction this unpredictable pendulum swings.

MATERIALS

- 2 chairs
- Broom
- Magnetic wand
- String
- Scissors
- Tape
- Other magnets and metallic objects from around the house

THE STEPS

1. Place the chairs on a level surface about 4 feet away from each other.

2. Suspend a broom between the seats of the chairs.

3. Tie a magnetic wand to the end of the string. If you don't have a magnetic wand, you can tape a bar magnet or a horseshoe magnet to the end of the string.

4. Tie the other end of the string to the broom handle so that the magnetic wand is about 12 inches off the ground. It should be close enough that it affects metal objects and other magnets that are the floor, but not so close that everything sticks right to it. Tape the string to the broom handle.

5. Arrange smaller magnets and metal objects on the floor beneath the wand magnet.

6. Pull the magnetic wand back and let it swing from side to side over the other magnets.

Observations What happens as the magnetic wand swings over the other magnets and metal objects?

Now Try This! Arrange the smaller magnets and metal objects into different shapes and patterns on the floor. Swing the magnetic wand in different directions, too. How does this change the effect?

> **The Hows and Whys** Without any outside forces, a pendulum will swing back and forth around its pivot forever. However, the magnetic attraction between the magnets and the metals make this pendulum swing and spin in unexpected and unpredictable ways.

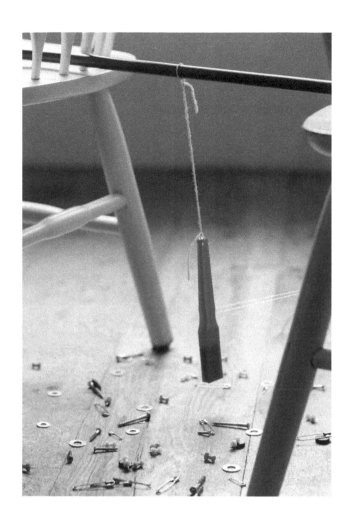

MAKE AN ELECTROMAGNET

LEVEL OF DIFFICULTY: MEDIUM
FROM BEGINNING TO END: 30 MINUTES
OTHER CATEGORIES: SCIENCE

(?) Electromagnets are found all around us. Electrical appliances, such as mechanical toothbrushes, doorbells, and electric lawnmowers, use magnets to turn energy into motion. Can you make your own electromagnet?

(!) *Caution: When the wires are connected to the battery, do not touch them. They will get hot as the electrical current runs through the wire. And never allow the wires of the electromagnet to get near a household outlet!*

MATERIALS
- 3 feet insulated copper wire
- Iron nail 3 to 6 inches long, or a long screwdriver
- Wire stripper
- Tape
- D battery
- Small metal objects, like paperclips, thumbtacks, and washers

THE STEPS

1. Wrap the wire tightly around the nail, making sure not to overlap the wires. Leave 6 to 8 inches of wire free on each side. The longer the nail and the more you wrap the wire, the better it works.

2. Use a wire stripper to remove about 1 inch of plastic coating from the wire on each end.

3. Secure a D battery to a table with a long piece of tape.

4. Attach one end of the wire to one end of the battery. Secure it with tape.

5. Attach the other end of the wire to the other end of the battery with tape. Be careful not to touch the exposed wire because it will get hot.

6. You have now created an electromagnet! Use the nail to pick up small metal objects. If it doesn't work, check that the wire is connected to the battery on each end and make sure you are using a fresh battery.

Observations How many paperclips or thumbtacks can you pick up with the nail?

Now Try This! Try creating an electromagnet using 2 batteries instead of just one. Connect the positive end of one battery to the negative end of another battery and then attach the wires onto the 2 outside ends of the batteries. Is the new electromagnet stronger? How many paperclips or thumbtacks can you pick up now?

The Hows and Whys An electrical circuit is created when a wire is connected to both ends of the battery, making an electrical current flow through the wire. This creates a magnetic field around the coiled wire, magnetizing the metal nail as if it were a permanent magnet. However, you can turn the magnet off by breaking the circuit and turn it back on by completing the circuit. This is how giant electromagnets at a scrapyard work to move scrap metal and junk cars.

TEA BAG HOT AIR BALLOON

LEVEL OF DIFFICULTY: EASY

FROM BEGINNING TO END: 10 MINUTES

OTHER CATEGORIES: SCIENCE

? How does a hot air balloon work? How does it fly in the air? Learn about air density by building and launching your own tea bag hot air balloon.

! *Caution:* *Be very careful with fire and matches. Ask an adult before you use them, and make sure you are in a fire-safe area.*

MATERIALS

- Tea bag with string attached
- Scissors
- Mug
- Glass plate
- Match

THE STEPS

1. Use scissors to cut the tea bag open on the side attached to the string. Dump the contents into a mug to use later or discard.

2. Shape the tea bag into a cylinder and stand it up on a glass plate.

3. Use a match to light the top of the tea bag on fire.

Observations What happens to the tea bag?

Now Try This! Shape other kinds of paper into a cylinder and see if it flies like the tea bag when it's lit on fire. Try printer paper, card stock, tissue paper, cardboard, and so on.

The Hows and Whys When air is heated, the air molecules move around quickly and spread out. This makes hot air rise because it is less dense than cold air. When the tea bag is lit on fire, it heats up the air inside and around the paper to such an extent that a warm air current lifts up the lightweight tea bag. A hot air balloon works the same way: by heating up trapped air in the balloon to make it fly above the ground.

MINI LIGHTNING SPARK

LEVEL OF DIFFICULTY: EASY
FROM BEGINNING TO END: 20 MINUTES

? Do you know how lightning is formed and what it is made of? In this science experiment, you will create your own small lightning spark to see how real lightning works. This may work best in a darkened room.

MATERIALS

- Aluminum pie tin
- Push pin or thumbtack
- Pencil with an eraser
- Foam plate
- Wool blanket

THE STEPS

1. Push a thumbtack through the center of the pie tin so the point is sticking out the back of the tin.

2. Push the pencil eraser through the pointy end of the thumbtack to create a handle for the pie tin.

3. Rub the foam plate vigorously for about 1 minute with wool or on your hair.

4. Touch the aluminum plate to the foam plate.

Observations What did you see when the aluminum plate touched the foam plate?

Now Try This! What other metal objects could you use to make the charge jump from the foam plate?

The Hows and Whys Rubbing the foam plate with wool gives it a static charge by transferring electrons from the wool to the foam plate. When you hold the pie tin near it, the charge jumps from the plate to the tin. You should see a tiny flash as the charge travels through the air.

Lightning works in a similar way. Within a thundercloud, millions of frozen raindrops bump into one another. This friction creates an electrical charge that builds up until the bottom of the thundercloud develops a negative charge, creating a positive charge on the ground below. The charge coming up from the ground eventually connects with the charge in the clouds and a lightning bolt strikes.

WINDMILL CHALLENGE

LEVEL OF DIFFICULTY: EASY
FROM BEGINNING TO END: 40 MINUTES
OTHER CATEGORIES: ENGINEERING

? A windmill is a machine that converts energy from the wind into useful work by rotating. Can you design a windmill that will do work?

MATERIALS

- Square piece of paper
- Hole puncher
- Scissors
- Tape
- Drinking straw
- String
- Paperclip
- Wooden skewer

THE STEPS

1. Fold the piece of paper in half diagonally (corner to corner). Unfold it and then fold it again diagonally the other direction.

2. Use a hole puncher to punch a hole in the center of the paper, right where the 2 creases intersect.

3. Use scissors to cut along the fold lines, stopping about ½ inch from the hole.

4. Bring every other point toward the center, right before the edge of the hole. Attach the 4 points there with tape.

5. Insert a straw through the center hole. Attach the pinwheel to the middle of the straw with tape.

6. Cut a piece of string about 2 feet long. Tape one end of the string to one end of the straw. Tie the other end of the string to a paperclip.

7. Insert a wooden skewer through the straw. Make sure the wooden skewer is longer than the straw and sticks out the ends.

8. Hold the ends of the wooden skewer and blow on the wheel. If nothing happens, try turning the windmill around and blowing on the other side.

Observations What happens when you blow on the windmill? Does it convert wind into work?

Now Try This! Try making the wheel from different kinds of paper and see which one works the most efficiently. Use heavier paper, like cardboard or card stock, and lighter paper, like tissue paper or printer paper, to compare how they each work to rotate the windmill.

The Hows and Whys In physics, work is done when an object is moved by a force over some distance. Windmills perform work by powering a generator that produces electricity through their rotation in the wind. Your windmill performs work by lifting the paperclip when you blow on the sails.

STRING TELEPHONE

LEVEL OF DIFFICULTY: EASY
FROM BEGINNING TO END: 45 MINUTES
OTHER CATEGORIES: SCIENCE

? How does sound travel? Can sound travel through solids? Make a tin can string telephone and experiment with sound while telling your best friend secrets from a distance.

! *Caution:* Ask an adult to help you sand down the rough spots around the edges of the tin cans and to hammer a nail through the bottoms of the tin cans.

MATERIALS

- 2 empty, clean tin cans
- Nail file or sandpaper
- Nail
- Hammer
- Fishing line
- Scissors
- 2 paper clips

THE STEPS

1. Use a nail file or sandpaper to file away any rough spots around the edges of the tin cans.

2. Turn the cans upside down. Hammer a nail through the center of the bottom of each and then pull the nail back out, leaving a hole. File away any sharp edges.

3. Use scissors to cut a piece of fishing line 10 to 60 feet long. The length will depend on where you will be using the telephone.

4. Poke each end of the fishing line through the hole from the bottom of each tin can.

5. Tie the fishing line to a paper clip inside each can so that it stays in place.

6. Grab one can while a friend takes the other one. Make sure the line is pulled tight and that it isn't touching anything else. Talk through your tin can while your friend listens, and then switch.

Observations How well can you hear your friend on the other end of the string telephone? What happens if the string goes slack in the middle?

Now Try This! Experiment by making a string telephone out of different kinds of string. Try twine, yarn, kite string, or cotton string. Compare how well they each work to transfer sound.

The Hows and Whys Sounds waves are simply vibrations. They travel much farther through liquids and solids than they do through air. In this activity, the sound waves from your voice vibrate the tin can, which vibrates the string. The vibrations are transferred across the string to your friend's tin can, where they vibrate the air particles. Your friend's ears detect the vibrating particles in the air as the sound of your voice.

Landline phones work in a similar way, but they convert the sound waves into an electrical signal, which can travel even farther over wires.

ZIP LINE CHALLENGE

LEVEL OF DIFFICULTY: EASY

FROM BEGINNING TO END: 40 MINUTES

OTHER CATEGORIES: ENGINEERING

 A zip line is made of a pulley suspended on a cable that is mounted on a slope. Can you build a zip line that will carry a trolley full of small toys?

Caution: *Ask an adult to help with the hot glue gun.*

MATERIALS

- Drinking straw
- Scissors
- Empty sewing bobbin
- Hot glue gun and glue sticks
- Coffee stirrer
- String or fishing line
- Small paper cup
- Masking tape
- Small toy or some coins

THE STEPS

1. Use scissors to trim a drinking straw so it's about 4 inches long.

2. Place the drinking straw through the hole in the center of the bobbin. Use hot glue to secure the bobbin to the middle of the drinking straw.

3. Place a coffee stirrer inside the drinking straw.

4. Cut 2 small holes on opposite sides of the cup, about 1 inch from the rim.

5. Cut a piece of string about 16 inches long. Thread one end through the coffee stirrer.

6. Thread the other end of the string through both holes in the paper cup and tie the 2 ends of the string together.

7. Cut another piece of string several feet long. Use tape to secure one side of the string to something a few feet off the ground, like a countertop or table.

8. Run the unattached end of the string between the bobbin and the cup, resting the bobbin on top of the string. Attach the end of the string to the ground or to the leg of a chair so that it is pulled tight.

9. Position the bobbin pulley at the top of the slope. Place a toy or some coins in the cup and let the trolley run down the line.

Observations How does the angle of the zip line affect how fast the pulley system travels? How much weight can the zip line carry?

Now Try This! Can you construct a zip line that will carry even more weight? What kinds of materials do you need to use?

The Hows and Whys Gravity pulls the trolley down the cable. Friction between the pulley and the cable as well as sag in the cable slow the trolley down.

Chapter four

ENGINEERING

Get ready to design and build incredible inventions!

In this chapter, you will build boats and cars that move on their own, construct parachutes and airplanes that really fly, and create unique roller coasters and mazes from simple supplies you probably already have in your house.

You'll be using lots of items from the recycle bin and a hot glue gun to build. You'll also be engineering a laser maze that requires the use of a laser pointer. This can be purchased for about $5 in the office supply section or the pet section of a grocery store. Lasers are often marketed as toys for dogs and cats to chase.

The activities in this chapter give you basic guidelines to follow, but feel free to diverge and create something new! If your Drinking Straw Roller Coaster (page 125) looks much different from the one in the book, that's the way it should be. Use your own creativity and ingenuity to build from the experiments and activities here.

As a novice engineer, however, there are a few guidelines you should keep in mind before you dive in.

First, always begin with the end in mind. What is the goal of building your project? Is it supposed to hold a certain amount of weight, drive a certain distance, or do something for a certain amount of time? Keeping the end goal in mind will help you design and build with focus.

Second, before you begin building, always use a paper and pencil to sketch out a quick blueprint of your design or to write down a few ideas you want to incorporate into it. This

will give you a good foundation to start with.

Third, don't be afraid to modify your design. Good engineers are constantly testing out their designs and making changes to improve them. As you test, retest, modify, build, and rebuild, you will maximize the functionality of your project and the fun in creating it.

Fourth, failure is not just normal, it is expected. If something you build collapses immediately, that's okay! Look for what went wrong, think through ways to improve the design, and try again. The struggle makes the victory at the end that much sweeter.

Last, remember to have a ton a fun as you create, problem solve, experiment, and build.

BALLOON CANNON

LEVEL OF DIFFICULTY: EASY
FROM BEGINNING TO END: 30 MINUTES

? Can you use a balloon to knock down a stack of cups 5 feet away? It may be harder than you think.

MATERIALS

- Paper or plastic cups
- Party balloons
- Clothespin or chip clip
- Tape
- Feathers, drinking straws, cardboard tubes, and/or card stock

THE STEPS

1. Set up the cups in a stacked pyramid.

2. Stand about 5 feet away. Inflate a balloon, aim it at the stack of cups, and let it fly. Did it knock down the pyramid?

3. Inflate the balloon again. Twist the neck and attach a clothespin to it to keep the balloon closed.

4. Use tape and your other materials to add wings or fins or a nose to the balloon. Aim it at the stack of cups, take off the clothespin, and see if it flies any straighter.

5. Keep experimenting and see if you can design a balloon cannon that will predictably shoot in a straight line.

Observations Does adding wings or fins or a nose to the balloon change its trajectory? Does it fly any straighter? Does the path of the balloon depend on the way or the location from which it is released?

Now Try This! Once you have mastered the balloon cannon from 5 feet, step back 10 feet from the cup pyramid and see if you can knock it down with the balloon from this distance.

The Hows and Whys A deflating balloon spins in circles because the air rushing out of it exits at an angle. Since the neck of the balloon is flexible, it wobbles with the force of the releasing air, causing it to rotate. In order for the balloon to fly in a straight line, the air rushing out of it has to create a force exactly in the center of the balloon.

BALLOON-POWERED CAR

LEVEL OF DIFFICULTY: MEDIUM
FROM BEGINNING TO END: 60 MINUTES
OTHER CATEGORIES: TECHNOLOGY, MATH

(?) Can you build a car that is propelled by nothing but a deflating balloon? Tap into the power of your own creativity as you design, build, and test a one-of-a-kind balloon-powered car. Learn about Newton's third law of motion, too.

(!) *Caution: Ask an adult to help with the hot glue gun and poking holes in the caps.*

MATERIALS

- Cardboard
- Ruler
- Scissors
- Drinking straws
- Tape
- Party balloon
- Wooden skewers
- Plastic caps (from milk jugs or water bottles)
- Hot glue gun and glue sticks

THE STEPS

1. Use a ruler and scissors to cut a piece of cardboard in a 3-by-6-inch rectangle. This is the body of the car.

2. Trim 2 straws so you have two 3-inch pieces. Attach them with tape to the cardboard rectangle so that they are parallel to each other and to the short sides of the rectangle. These will hold the axles.

3. Fit the mouth of a balloon over another straw. Tape it securely and make sure it is airtight, and then tape this straw lengthwise onto the top of the car.

4. Slide the skewers through the 2 parallel straws. These are the axles.

5. Poke each end of each skewer through the center of a plastic cap. These are the wheels. Make sure the wheel is attached well to the skewer, using hot glue if needed.

6. Inflate the balloon by blowing into its straw. Pinch the straw, set the car on a smooth surface, and let the straw go!

Observations How far does the car go before it stops? Does it go in a straight line? What adjustments do you need to make?

Now Try This! Build more balloon-powered cars using different materials and measure how far they each go. You are limited only by your imagination! Some ideas to try:

- **For the base:** cardboard tube, plastic water bottle, plastic cup, or a piece of foam
- **For the axles:** pencils, sticks, or skewers
- **For the wheels:** CDs, empty rolls of tape, or LEGO wheels

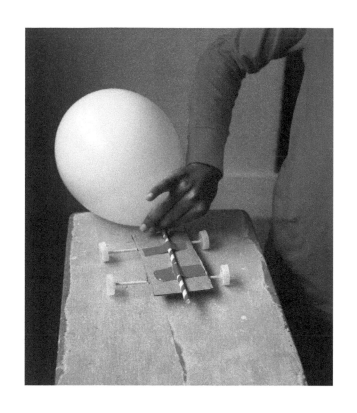

The Hows and Whys Building a balloon-powered car is a wonderful illustration of Newton's third law of motion: for every action, there is an equal but opposite reaction. The action is the air rushing from the straw and pushing against the air behind the car. The reaction is the air behind the car pushing against the car with the same force, causing the forward movement of the car.

CRAFT STICK BRIDGE

LEVEL OF DIFFICULTY: EASY
FROM BEGINNING TO END: 45 MINUTES

? Can you make a bridge out of materials like craft sticks, binder clips, or clothespins that holds a significant amount of weight? Experiment with different designs, different shapes, and various materials to see how you can create a very strong bridge.

MATERIALS
- Pencil and paper
- Jumbo craft sticks
- Binder clips
- Clothespins
- 2 chairs
- Several books

THE STEPS

1. Use a pencil and paper to sketch out a plan of what you want the bridge to look like.

2. Secure craft sticks together with binder clips and clothespins to build a freestanding bridge. Suspend the bridge between the seats of the chairs.

3. When your structure is complete, pile books on top of it, one by one. Count how many books it holds before it collapses.

Observations How many books did your structure hold? Did the result surprise you? Are there shapes or methods of building that are stronger than others?

Now Try This! Continue building with these materials to make more structures. How high can you build a craft stick tower before it falls over? Pile books on top of your other creations to see how strong they are.

The Hows and Whys You may notice that many bridges in real life are constructed using triangular shapes. This is because triangles are cross-braced, so they support side and top loads well. It is also economical to build using triangles because fewer materials can be used to support very heavy loads.

LASER MAZE

LEVEL OF DIFFICULTY: EASY
FROM BEGINNING TO END: 30 MINUTES
OTHER CATEGORIES: TECHNOLOGY, MATH

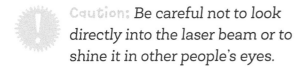 Can you direct a laser beam to a target using mirrors? Experiment with mirrors and angles of reflection by making a fun laser maze.

Caution: *Be careful not to look directly into the laser beam or to shine it in other people's eyes.*

MATERIALS
- Piece of paper
- Markers
- Tape
- 3 small mirrors
- 6 binder clips
- Laser pointer (you can find one for about $5 at the grocery store in the office supply section or the pet section)
- Book
- Protractor

THE STEPS

1. Use markers to draw a small target on a piece of paper. Tape it to the wall.

2. Onto each mirror, attach 2 binder clips to act as "legs" so the mirror can stand up on its own and be adjusted easily.

3. Rest the laser pointer on a book and shine it into a mirror. Experiment with the angle of the mirror to see where the laser beam is reflected.

4. Set up the mirrors to reflect the laser around a maze so that it eventually hits the target on the wall.

5. After you do one maze, move the starting position of the laser and create a new maze to hit the target again.

Observations At what angles are the mirrors positioned in relation to the laser beam? Use a protractor to find out. See if you can predict where the beam will be reflected.

Now Try This! Can you make a maze using 4 mirrors?

The Hows and Whys The laser pointer emits a very narrow, low-powered beam of visible light that is reflected off the mirrors at an angle dependent on the angle of the mirror itself.

DRINKING STRAW ROLLER COASTER

LEVEL OF DIFFICULTY: MEDIUM
FROM BEGINNING TO END: 60 MINUTES

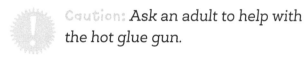 Can you build a ping-pong ball roller coaster out of drinking straws? Can you keep the ball rolling continuously for 10 seconds? Gather up a few household supplies and send your ping-pong ball on a wild ride.

Caution: *Ask an adult to help with the hot glue gun.*

MATERIALS

- Paper and pencil
- Cardboard box
- Drinking straws
- Hot glue gun and glue sticks
- Ping-pong ball

THE STEPS

1. Use paper and a pencil to plan out and sketch a fun roller coaster for the ping-pong ball to follow.

2. Using a cardboard box as a base, begin building the roller coaster by attaching straws to it with hot glue. Remember to use 2 parallel straws as the track to hold the ball.

3. Before gluing, test each section out with the ball to make sure the angles work and the track is narrow enough to hold the ball and wide enough that the ball won't fall off easily.

4. Perform several test runs and modify the roller coaster as needed.

Observations Were there sections of the roller coaster you had to modify from your original plans for it to work?

Now Try This! Can you make an even bigger roller coaster out of drinking straws? Can you reinforce your roller coaster so that it is strong enough for a golf ball to travel down it?

The Hows and Whys Gravity pulls the ping-pong ball down the track, but it will travel faster or slower depending on the angle of the track and the amount of friction the ball experiences against the straws.

MARBLE RUN GAME

 Can you create a marble run out of a cardboard box and craft sticks? Can you keep the marble moving for 10 seconds or more? Create a cool game and experiment with gravity at the same time.

Caution: *Ask an adult to help with the hot glue gun.*

MATERIALS

- Pencil and paper
- Large cardboard box
- Jumbo craft sticks
- Scissors
- Hot glue gun and glue sticks
- Pipe cleaners
- Pom-poms
- Paper cups
- Marbles

THE STEPS

1. Use a pencil and paper to plan out the design of your marble run.

2. Disassemble the cardboard box so that it lies flat.

3. Use scissors to trim the craft sticks, and use a hot glue gun to attach the craft sticks to the cardboard, flat-side down, to make a path.

4. Make different obstacles and traps using pipe cleaners, pom-poms, and other craft supplies.

5. Attach paper cups to the bottom of the marble run to catch the marbles.

6. Prop the marble run against a couch or table at an angle and test it out with a few marbles. Make adjustments and have fun playing!

Observations Did the marbles get evenly distributed among the cups at the bottom? Why do you think this happened?

Now Try This! Try running other small balls down the marble run and compare them to the marbles. Some ideas to try include pom-poms, bouncy balls, and ping-pong balls.

The Hows and Whys Gravity pulls the marbles down, but the angles of the craft sticks will determine how fast the marbles roll.

EGG DROP CHALLENGE

LEVEL OF DIFFICULTY: MEDIUM
FROM BEGINNING TO END: 60 MINUTES

? Can you construct a container that will protect a raw egg from cracking when dropped from a height? Raid the recycle bin and the craft closet to design and build your own unique contraption. The possibilities are endless to complete this fun engineering challenge. The creations are as unique as the people who create them!

 Caution: *Wash your hands with soap and water after touching raw eggs.*

MATERIALS

- Pencil and paper
- Various household materials, like craft sticks, plastic containers, rubber bands, straws, tape, scissors, hot glue, plastic bags, sponges, bubble wrap, newspaper, cardboard tubes, string, and balloons
- Eggs

THE STEPS

1. Take a few minutes to plan your protective egg machine, using a pencil and paper to sketch it out. Take into account the materials you have available (and have permission to use), the height from which you plan to drop it, and the principles of science you already know.

2. Construct your egg drop container with the materials you've chosen, keeping in mind that you will have to be able to insert an egg into it easily.

3. When it is finished, head to the top of a play structure or a balcony and drop your invention with an egg inside.

Observations Did the egg crack? What improvements can you make to your design?

Now Try This! If your egg survived the first drop, try dropping it from a greater height, if possible. Or try throwing the egg drop machine up into the air rather than just dropping it. Did the egg crack?

The Hows and Whys Gravity pulls the egg down, but by insulating the egg or finding ways to slow down its fall, it doesn't break when it hits the ground.

LEVITATING PING-PONG BALL

LEVEL OF DIFFICULTY: EASY
FROM BEGINNING TO END: 15 MINUTES
OTHER CATEGORIES: SCIENCE

? Can you make a ping-pong ball magically levitate in the air? Use just a few simple supplies to complete this cool science trick and learn all about air pressure.

MATERIALS

- Cone-shaped paper cup
- Scissors
- Bendable drinking straw
- Tape
- Ping-pong ball

THE STEPS

1. Use scissors to cut the tip off of a cone-shaped paper cup.

2. Insert the short end of a bendable drinking straw into the hole from the bottom of the cup.

3. Securely tape the straw and the cup together. Bend the straw 90 degrees so you can hold it horizontally and keep the cup upright.

4. Place a ping-pong ball into the cone. Blow into the long end of the straw and watch what happens!

Observations What happens when you blow air into the straw? How hard do you have to blow to get the ball to levitate?

Now Try This! What happens if you use a longer or a wider straw?

The Hows and Whys Bernoulli's principle states that if air speeds up, the pressure is lowered. The air that you are blowing around the sides of the ping-pong ball is moving quickly, which means it's at a lower pressure than the surrounding, stationary air. Gravity pulls the ping-pong ball downward while the air blowing from below the ping-pong ball forces it upward. When all the forces acting on the ping-pong ball are balanced, it hovers in midair.

PADDLEBOAT

LEVEL OF DIFFICULTY: EASY
FROM BEGINNING TO END: 30 MINUTES

(?) Can you make a paddleboat that moves through the water using its own power? Raid the recycle bin, construct a paddleboat, and learn how real steamboats work.

MATERIALS

- Shallow plastic storage container or disposable plastic water bottle laid on its side
- 2 pencils
- Duct tape
- Rubber band
- Plastic milk jug
- Scissors
- Pool or bathtub full of water

THE STEPS

1. Attach each pencil to opposite sides of the plastic container with duct tape. Attach them about ¾ of the way down the container, leaving about 4 inches of each pencil free in the back.

2. Wrap a rubber band around the free ends of the pencils.

3. Construct the paddle: Use scissors to cut out 4 equal rectangles from a plastic milk jug, then fold each rectangle in half and arrange them into a cross shape with all the folds touching in the middle.

4. Use duct tape to attach one end of each rectangle to one end of another rectangle so that the cross holds its shape.

5. Slide one blade of the paddle through the rubber band on the boat.

6. Wind up the paddle. Set the boat in a pool or bathtub and let the paddle go!

Observations In what direction does the boat travel? Does it move in a straight line or does its path curve? How can you improve the boat's performance?

Now Try This! Adjust the position of the paddle either closer to or farther away from the boat to see if it changes how the paddle-boat is propelled. Does it make a difference whether the paddle is twisted forward or backward?

The Hows and Whys When the paddle is wound, the rubber band twists. The twisted rubber band stores potential energy that is converted to kinetic energy when it unwinds. As the rubber band unwinds, the paddle blades act as oars, pushing against the water as they rotate. This propels the boat through the water.

PAN FLUTE

LEVEL OF DIFFICULTY: EASY
FROM BEGINNING TO END: 20 MINUTES
OTHER CATEGORIES: ART, MATH

? Can you make a musical instrument using a few drinking straws and tape? Experiment with pitch and learn how sound is made by simply blowing air through a straw.

MATERIALS

- Drinking straws
- Ruler
- Scissors
- Tape

THE STEPS

1. Line up 7 to 10 drinking straws on a smooth surface. Leave the first straw alone and then use a ruler and scissors to trim ½ inch from the second straw. Cut off 1 inch from the third straw, 1½ inches from the fourth straw, and so on, cutting an additional ½ inch from each successive straw.

2. Place a long piece of tape on a smooth surface with the sticky side up.

3. Arrange the straws on the tape from longest to shortest, with the tops of the straws flush in a line.

4. Fold the tape over the straws and secure it on the other side.

5. Play the pan flute by holding the straight edge of the straws up and blowing air across the top of the straws.

Observations Which straw makes the highest pitch? The lowest? Is there a relationship between the length of the straw and the sound that comes out of it?

Now Try This! Experiment with the pan flute to try to play a simple song, like "Mary Had a Little Lamb" or "Jingle Bells." Do you need to add more straws?

The Hows and Whys Sound is produced by the vibration of air blowing across the open hole at the end of a resonating tube. This is the same way that sound is produced through a trumpet or a recorder.

PAPER CONE FLIERS

LEVEL OF DIFFICULTY: EASY

FROM BEGINNING TO END: 20 MINUTES

 Can you design a flier out of a paper cone that levitates in the air for more than 5 seconds?

MATERIALS

- Blow dryer
- Books, boxes, or stools
- Cone-shaped paper cups
- Scissors
- Tape
- Craft supplies, like feathers, pipe cleaners, and pom-poms

THE STEPS

1. Set up a blow dryer so that it blows air upward. Rest it between 2 piles of books, boxes, or stools and prop up the nozzle as needed to keep the air blowing upward.

2. Use scissors to cut slits along the edge of a cone-shaped paper cup and/or cut the tip off. Fold the paper cup, tape other crafting supplies to it, or just leave it as is.

3. Turn on the blow dryer and let the paper flier go in the airstream.

4. Count how long it levitates in the airstream. Make adjustments, create new fliers, and see which design works the best!

Observations Which designs keep the paper flier levitating the longest in the airstream? Do the best fliers have anything in common?

Now Try This! Take the best flier and try adding weight to it. Tape a few coins to it and see if it continues to fly as well as it did before. What new modifications need to be made?

PARACHUTE FLIERS

LEVEL OF DIFFICULTY: EASY
FROM BEGINNING TO END: 30 MINUTES
OTHER CATEGORIES: MATH

? Can you design a parachute that transports small objects to the ground safely? Gather up a few simple supplies, build a parachute, and learn all about air resistance and gravity.

MATERIALS

- Small plastic or paper cup
- Hole puncher
- String
- Scissors
- Plastic grocery bag
- Stopwatch
- Small toys, like army figures and bouncy balls, or coins

THE STEPS

1. Use a hole puncher to punch 4 equidistant holes along the top rim of a cup.

2. Use scissors to cut 4 lengths of string, each about 14 inches long.

3. Cut a plastic grocery bag into a 14-inch square.

4. Tie one end of each string to a corner of the square. Tie the other end of each string through a hole in the cup. Try to keep each piece of string equally long so that you don't make a lopsided parachute.

5. Stand on a high place, like a deck, a play structure, or a balcony, and drop your parachute.

6. Use a stopwatch to time how long the parachute takes to hit the ground.

7. If it is gliding well, load up the cup with small toys and see how long it takes the loaded parachute to reach the ground from the same height.

CONTINUED ➡

Observations How long does an empty parachute take to glide to the ground? How about a loaded one? Is there a relationship between the weight of the parachute and how long it takes to hit the ground?

Now Try This! Vary the lengths of the strings and the size of the parachute to see what happens. Can you design a parachute that will hold more weight or descend more slowly?

The Hows and Whys When air gets under the plastic grocery bag, it exerts an upward force against the parachute. This is called air resistance. It's the same force that enables a leaf to gently flutter to the ground or a piece of paper to be swept up in the wind.

PAPER AIRPLANE CHALLENGE

LEVEL OF DIFFICULTY: EASY
FROM BEGINNING TO END: 30 MINUTES
OTHER CATEGORIES: MATH

? Can you construct a paper airplane that glides 10 feet while carrying weight? This creative engineering challenge is fun, engaging, and educational all at the same time.

MATERIALS

- Construction paper
- Tape measure
- Tape
- Coins

THE STEPS

1. Fold a piece of construction paper into a paper airplane. Use the Internet to research how to fold a paper airplane if you don't already know how.

2. Decide on a starting line and measure 10 feet away from that line using a tape measure.

3. Throw the paper airplane forward and see if it glides at least 10 feet. Fold more paper airplanes and make modifications to make them fly farther.

4. Tape coins to the airplanes and measure how far they fly with weight attached. Keep track of the results on a table.

Observations How many coins can you attach to your paper airplane and still make it fly 10 feet?

Now Try This! Modify your designs to see if you can construct an airplane that flies farther or straighter with weight attached.

The Hows and Whys Similar to jumbo jets, paper airplanes fly because of a few different factors. An airplane needs thrust, or energy, to move it forward. This is supplied by your arm. It also needs lift to stay in the air. Lift happens because the air pressure is greater underneath the wings than it is on top of the wings, enabling even very heavy airplanes to glide effortlessly through the air.

POM-POM DROP

LEVEL OF DIFFICULTY: EASY

FROM BEGINNING TO END: 30 MINUTES

OTHER CATEGORIES: MATH

(?) Can you make a pom-pom drop course that will keep the pom-pom rolling for 10 seconds or more? Learn about gravity, experiment with different angles, and get a hands-on lesson in friction and momentum while building a fun tube slide on the wall.

MATERIALS

- Pencil and paper
- Several cardboard tubes from paper towels, toilet paper, or wrapping paper
- Wall-safe tape, like masking tape or painter's tape
- Scissors
- Pom-poms
- Stopwatch

THE STEPS

1. Use a pencil and paper to sketch out your design for a pom-pom drop course.

2. Tape the cardboard tubes to the wall, using the scissors to trim and cut the tubes as necessary.

3. Drop a pom-pom through the course and time it with a stopwatch to see how long it takes to get from the top to the bottom.

Observations How long did the pom-pom take to get through the course? What can you do to make it go faster? To make it go slower?

Now Try This! Drop heavier balls, like marbles or bouncy balls, through the pom-pom drop course. Time how long they each take to get through the course and compare the results. Are they different? Why?

The Hows and Whys Gravity is the force that pulls objects to the Earth. Even though gravity constantly pulls the pom-pom down, it will travel faster or slower depending on the angles of the cardboard tubes. A steeper angle will allow the pom-pom to go faster and gain momentum as it rolls through the course.

PULLEY SYSTEM

LEVEL OF DIFFICULTY: EASY

FROM BEGINNING TO END: 30 MINUTES

? Can you engineer a pulley that can lift a heavy load? Learn how this simple machine works to lift and lower objects and experiment to see how much weight it can move.

MATERIALS

- 2 cardboard tubes from paper towel rolls
- Scissors
- Long pencil
- Empty spool of ribbon
- Masking tape
- Small paper cup
- Yarn
- Small objects, like cereal, plastic toys, or paper clips

THE STEPS

1. Carefully use scissors to poke a hole big enough for a pencil to fit through in a cardboard tube, about 2 inches from the end. Poke another hole directly opposite the first hole. Do the same with the other tube.

2. Fit the pencil through the center hole of the empty spool of ribbon.

3. Insert one end of the pencil through the holes in one cardboard tube and the other end of the pencil through the holes in the other cardboard tube so that about an inch of pencil hangs out each side.

4. Tape the cardboard tubes upright to a flat surface with the pencil at the top.

5. Use scissors to poke 2 holes opposite each other just below the rim of the cup.

6. Thread a piece of yarn through the holes and tie it together to give the cup a short bucket handle.

7. Cut another piece of yarn about 3 feet long and attach one end to the handle. Thread the other end over the ribbon spool pulley.

8. Load up the cup with some lightweight objects. Pull the end of the yarn to lift the cup using your pulley system.

Observations How much weight can your pulley system lift? Are there any adjustments you need to make so that the system is more sturdy?

Now Try This! Can you add more pulleys to your system? Does adding more pulleys affect how much weight the system can move?

The Hows and Whys A pulley is a simple machine that uses grooved wheels and a rope to raise, lower, or move a load. Using a pulley reverses the direction of the lifting force, making it easier to move a load. With a pulley, you can pull the yarn down to move the load up!

SNACK STRUCTURES

LEVEL OF DIFFICULTY: EASY
FROM BEGINNING TO END: 20 MINUTES

Who says you shouldn't play with your food? In this experiment, we are going to turn snack time into building time! Get creative and see how tall you can build a grape tower, how sturdy you can make a cheese hut, and how intricate you can create an apple mansion.

MATERIALS
- Pencil and paper
- Toothpicks
- Small finger foods, such as grapes, sliced apples, berries, cheese cubes, raisins, and marshmallows
- Plate

THE STEPS

1. Use a pencil and paper to sketch out a design of what your snack structure is going to look like. Make a plan for building it. Consider such questions as, What kind of base do I build? Which foods can be placed over or under other foods?

2. Use toothpicks to connect different finger foods together. Construct walls, a ceiling, and decorations.

3. On a plate, put it all together into one big snack structure.

Observations Did you have to modify your original plans in any way? Why?

Now Try This! Add on to your structure to make it bigger, taller, and more stable.

The Hows and Whys You may find that reinforcing your snack structure with toothpicks to make triangular shapes will make it more sturdy. This is because triangles are cross-braced, so they support side and top loads well.

STRONG SHAPES

LEVEL OF DIFFICULTY: EASY

FROM BEGINNING TO END: 20 MINUTES

OTHER CATEGORIES: MATH

? How strong is one piece of paper? Find out by seeing how many books it can hold. Fold the paper into different shapes and see if one geometrical shape is stronger than the others.

MATERIALS
- Printer paper
- Tape
- Books

THE STEPS

1. Make one piece of paper a cylinder by rolling it up and taping the sides together.

2. Fold a second piece of paper into a triangular prism by folding the paper lengthwise into thirds. Stand the paper up and tape the open sides together.

3. Fold a third piece of paper into a rectangular prism by folding the paper lengthwise in half and then lengthwise in half again so that there are 3 long creases. Stand the paper up and shape it into a rectangular prism. Tape the open sides together.

4. Test the strength of each column by placing the same books on each one in the same order. Keep track on a table of how many books each column holds before it collapses under the weight.

Observations Which of your columns held the most books? Why do you think that is?

Now Try This! Does it matter how tall each column is? Use smaller paper to make columns of the same shapes to see if there is a difference in their strength.

The Hows and Whys The force of the book pushing down is distributed around all of the edges of the paper. Since a cylinder has no corners, all parts of it are able to distribute the weight of the book evenly. In most cases, this means that the cylinder can hold the most books before collapsing, though your results may be different depending on how tightly each of your columns was constructed.

STRAW PLANE

LEVEL OF DIFFICULTY: EASY

FROM BEGINNING TO END: 15 MINUTES

OTHER CATEGORIES: MATH

? Can you construct a paper flier using 2 rectangles of paper and a straw? Find out how far this flying machine can glide and modify it to see if you can improve your design.

MATERIALS

- Piece of card stock
- Ruler
- Scissors
- Tape
- Drinking straw

THE STEPS

1. Use a ruler and scissors to cut out 2 strips of card stock, the first one measuring 1 inch wide by 10 inches long and the second one measuring 1 inch wide by 5 inches long.

2. Tape the ends of the first strip together to make a circle. Do the same with the second strip.

3. Attach each circle shape to a straw.

4. Throw the flier as you would a paper airplane and see how far it flies.

Observations How does the straw plane fly differently if you launch it with the big circle in front compared with when you launch it with the small circle in front?

Now Try This! Modify the design to maximize the distance it flies. Move the circle shapes into different positions along the straw, modify the length of the strips of paper, experiment with the length of the straw, and see what happens if you add a third circle to the straw. Can you add some weight, like paperclips, to it and still make it fly?

The Hows and Whys Air moves through both the straw and the paper circles to enable the straw plane to fly. They act similarly to the wings of a paper airplane by providing lift.

SPINNING TOP

LEVEL OF DIFFICULTY: EASY

FROM BEGINNING TO END: 30 MINUTES

Tops were some of the first toys invented thousands of years ago. Can you design and build your own spinning top? Use materials from around the house and in the recycle bin to build several different models, experiment with size and placement of the spindle and the body, and see which tops spin the longest. All you will need to make is a spindle and a body for your top. There is no limit to what you can use!

Caution: *Ask an adult to help with the hot glue gun.*

MATERIALS

- Toothpick, penny, wooden skewer, crayon, or marker (for the spindle)
- Yogurt cup lid, milk jug cap, circular piece of cardboard, CD, or metal washer (for the body)
- Hot glue gun and glue sticks

THE STEPS

1. Choose which materials you want to use to build your top. You need a spindle and body. The body needs to be a circle with a small hole in the center for the spindle to fit through.

2. Fit the spindle through the body. Attach the 2 parts with hot glue.

3. Spin your top on a smooth, flat surface.

CONTINUED ➡

Observations Does a heavy body make the top spin longer than a light one does? How does the position of the body (higher or lower on the spindle) affect how the top spins?

Now Try This! Try making a top with 2 bodies. Does it spin better or worse? Does it make a difference if the bodies are the same size or different sizes?

The Hows and Whys A top spins rapidly on the ground, balanced on its tip, because of its rotational inertia. After spinning upright, the angular momentum of the top decreases due to friction, and it eventually topples.

STRAW RAFTS

LEVEL OF DIFFICULTY: EASY
FROM BEGINNING TO END: 30 MINUTES

 Can you use drinking straws to construct a raft that holds weight? Use a few simple supplies to make rafts that actually float and test them to see which design holds the most pennies before it sinks.

Caution: *Ask an adult to help with the hot glue gun.*

MATERIALS

- Pencil and paper
- Drinking straws
- Hot glue gun and glue sticks
- Scissors
- Large bowl of water (or a bathtub full of water)
- Pennies

THE STEPS

1. Take a few minutes to plan out a drinking straw raft design using a pencil and paper.

2. Using 5 drinking straws, scissors, and hot glue, construct a raft that floats in a bowl of water.

3. Test how many pennies it can hold before it sinks.

4. Modify the design and build new designs to see if one raft can hold more weight than the others.

Observations Did you have to modify your design? Why? How many pennies does your raft hold?

Now Try This! Can you match the number of pennies your raft holds by making another raft, this time using only 4 straws? How about 3 straws?

> **The Hows and Whys** Drinking straws are more buoyant than water, meaning they float on top. However, with added weight, gravity works against buoyancy, and eventually the raft sinks.

Chapter Five

Pull out your paintbrush and get ready to create amazing art with the power of science!

In this chapter, you will see sound waves, create a rainbow with dissolving candy, produce fizzy patterns with a pendulum, and engineer your own coloring robot!

Art is so much more than just drawing on a piece of paper. Art is using your imagination to create, build, and design something unique. It is dreaming up new ways to express yourself by experimenting with mediums and canvases that haven't been used before.

Science and art are intimately connected. Both a scientist and an artist have to possess a wild imagination to help them creatively solve problems. They both experiment through trial and error to push the boundaries of what is possible and to shatter those boundaries with creative breakthroughs.

In this chapter, you will use the principles of science to create art.

Always begin with a question: What happens if I mix these colors? How can I make different patterns? What materials can I use to make the ideas I imagine a reality?

Next, formulate a hypothesis using the same sentence you use when doing a science experiment: "I think . . . because . . ." This will help you discover new knowledge that sparks new ideas and more questions.

The really fun part comes next: experimenting. Find out what you can create, figure out the constraints you have, and then use your knowledge and creativity to fabricate something completely new. Experiment with patterns, colors, sounds, and light. Use the ideas and activities in this book to come up with your own scientific art experiments and projects.

After you are done experimenting and creating, state some conclusions. Remember the things you learned through your observations and creations.

Have a ton of fun experimenting with vibrant colors, unique patterns, new mediums, and unexpected canvases to produce something only you can create.

BUBBLE PAINTING

LEVEL OF DIFFICULTY: EASY
FROM BEGINNING TO END: 10 MINUTES

 Can you paint with bubbles? Sure you can! Blow bubbles to your heart's content, learn what bubbles are made of, and create interesting, colorful patterns in the process.

Caution: *Bubble painting can be very fun and messy. Wear clothes that you don't mind getting paint on.*

MATERIALS

- Small cup
- 2 tablespoons tempera paint
- 1 tablespoon water
- 2 tablespoons liquid dish soap
- Plate
- Drinking straw
- White paper
- Measuring spoons

THE STEPS

1. Mix the paint, water, and dish soap together in a cup.

2. Place the cup on a plate to catch the bubble overflow.

3. Place a drinking straw into the cup and blow through it to create bubbles being careful not to inhale or sip up any liquid.

4. Blow bubbles until the cup overflows.

5. Remove the straw, and carefully lay a piece of paper on top of the bubbles in the cup to make bubble prints.

Observations What kinds of patterns are created on the paper?

Now Try This! Use different sizes of straws to blow bubbles in the paint solution. Does a jumbo straw make different bubble prints than a coffee stirrer does?

The Hows and Whys The membrane of the actual bubbles is clear and can't be colored. However, when the bubbles pop, there is water and paint inside them that gets transferred to your paper. This creates unique bubble prints that you can layer with different colors and patterns.

CANDY RAINBOW

LEVEL OF DIFFICULTY: EASY
FROM BEGINNING TO END: 10 MINUTES
OTHER CATEGORIES: SCIENCE

? Can you create art using candy and water? Experiment with color mixing, vary the water temperature, and enjoy a sweet treat at the end.

MATERIALS
- Skittles candy
- White plate
- Hot tap water

THE STEPS

1. Arrange several Skittles on the plate. You can arrange them in a pattern or just place them randomly on the plate to see what happens.

2. Carefully pour hot water onto the center of the plate. Add just enough to cover the bottoms of the candies.

3. Wait a couple of minutes for your masterpiece to develop.

4. Observe your creation and then create another one. Vary the temperature of the water each time to see how the water temperature affects the speed of the reaction.

Observations What happened to the Skittles after the water was added? What patterns were produced? What new colors appeared?

Now Try This! Experiment with other candies to see if they react the same way that Skittles do in hot water. Candies to try include Nerds, M&M's, peppermints, jelly beans, gummy bears, or gobstoppers.

The Hows and Whys The colored coating on Skittles is made of sugar, which dissolves in water. As the water moves around the plate, the colored sugar moves along with it, creating brilliant patterns and rainbows. Notice how the primary colors mix to create new colors.

FIZZY PENDULUM SWING

LEVEL OF DIFFICULTY: EASY
FROM BEGINNING TO END: 60 MINUTES
OTHER CATEGORIES: SCIENCE, ENGINEERING

? Can you build a pendulum and use it to create beautiful textured art? Add a fizzy chemical reaction and you're set to have some real fun!

! *Caution: This fun experiment definitely gets messy! Be sure to do it outside where you can wash it away easily when you are done.*

MATERIALS
- Paper or plastic cup
- Hole puncher
- Pushpin
- String
- Scissors
- 2 chairs
- Broom
- Baking soda
- Tape
- Vinegar
- Food coloring

THE STEPS

1. Use a hole puncher to punch 3 equidistant holes about an inch below the rim of a cup.

2. Use a pushpin to poke a small hole in the center of the bottom of the cup.

3. Use scissors to cut 3 pieces of string about 8 inches long. Thread 1 piece through each of the holes you punched around the cup. Tie all the ends of the strings together in the center.

4. Head outside to a level piece of sidewalk or driveway. Set up the chairs about 4 feet apart with the backs facing each other.

5. Slide the broom through the backs of the chairs.

6. Cut another piece of string and attach it from the middle of the broom handle to the strings on the cup. The cup should be hanging about 12 inches off the ground.

7. Sprinkle a few cups of baking soda on the ground directly under and around the suspended cup.

8. Place a piece of tape on the outside of the cup over the hole in the bottom.

9. Fill the cup about halfway full of vinegar. Add a few drops of food coloring.

10. Pull the cup back, remove the tape from the bottom, and let it swing freely over the baking soda.

11. When the cup stops swinging, pull it back again to create a new pattern. Continue to refill it with colored vinegar until your masterpiece is complete!

Observations What happens as the cup swings over the baking soda? What do you notice about the reaction between baking soda and vinegar?

Now Try This! Add a little bit of liquid dish soap to the colored vinegar. How does this affect the reaction between baking soda and vinegar?

The Hows and Whys Without any friction, a pendulum will continue swinging exactly the same distance back and forth forever. However, since this simple pendulum creates lots of friction between the string and the broom handle, it slows down quickly. As it slows, the distance it swings decreases, producing really beautiful orbit-like patterns.

ICE COLOR MIXING

LEVEL OF DIFFICULTY: EASY
FROM BEGINNING TO END: 6 HOURS

? Can you make new colors from 2 existing ones? Create interesting colors and patterns while learning about freezing, melting, and color mixing.

MATERIALS

- Ice cube tray
- Water
- Food coloring
- White plates
- Spoons

THE STEPS

1. Fill the ice cube tray with water. Make different-colored ice cubes by dripping about 5 drops of food coloring into each compartment. (Be sure you make a few ice cubes of each of the primary colors: red, yellow, and blue.)

2. Leave the ice cube tray in the freezer for several hours.

3. Once the colored ice cubes are frozen, take them out of the freezer.

4. Place 2 different-colored ice cubes on each plate.

5. Have fun pushing the melting colored ice around the plate with a spoon to make different patterns.

Observations What new color is produced when 2 colored ice cubes melt together?

Now Try This! Experiment to see what happens when 2 primary colors are mixed together. What happens when all 3 primary colors are mixed together? What color is made when 2 secondary colors are mixed?

The Hows and Whys The ice melts into colored water. When the colored water mixes, a new color is produced.

DANCING PAPER

LEVEL OF DIFFICULTY: EASY
FROM BEGINNING TO END: 15 MINUTES
OTHER CATEGORIES: SCIENCE, TECHNOLOGY

? Can you see sound waves? Most of the time the answer is probably no, but in this artistic science experiment, you will get to actually see how sound waves move through the air.

MATERIALS

- Glass bowl
- Plastic wrap
- Tape or rubber band
- Tissue paper
- Any speaker you have access to, such as a TV speaker, the speaker in a laptop, or a wireless speaker

THE STEPS

1. Stretch plastic wrap tightly over the bowl. Secure it with tape or a rubber band.

2. Wad up a few small pieces of tissue paper and place them on the plastic wrap.

3. Set the bowl next to a speaker on a hard surface. The bigger the speaker, the better.

4. Turn some music on. Start with the volume down and gradually turn it up.

Observations What happens to the tissue paper as you increase the music volume? What style of music produces the best results?

Now Try This! Fill the bowl up with water and place it next to the speaker. Turn up the volume and play songs with a strong bass beat. What happens to the water?

The Hows and Whys Sound is a type of energy produced by vibrating particles in the air. Sound travels through the air in waves, which get stronger as the volume is turned up. When the music is loud enough, it causes the plastic wrap to vibrate, which you can observe as the little pieces of paper dance around on the surface.

MAGIC MILK

LEVEL OF DIFFICULTY: EASY
FROM BEGINNING TO END: 20 MINUTES
OTHER CATEGORIES: SCIENCE

(?) Can you turn a plate of milk into a gorgeous art canvas? Use food coloring and a drop of science magic to create beautiful swirling colors and firework patterns.

MATERIALS

- Plate or baking dish
- Milk
- Food coloring
- Liquid dish soap

THE STEPS

1. Pour a thin layer of milk onto a plate.

2. Drip a few drops of food coloring into the milk.

3. Carefully drip one drop of liquid dish soap into the milk.

Observations What kinds of patterns do the colors make? How do the colors move through the milk?

Now Try This! Experiment to see if the type of milk makes a difference in how the colors burst. Does whole milk work better than skim milk? How about heavy cream or soy milk?

The Hows and Whys The molecules at the surface of liquid bond tightly together. This is called surface tension. When dish soap is dripped onto the surface of the milk, the soap breaks the surface tension and the molecules on the surface spread out. Of course, the milk molecules take the food coloring with them, making them look like exploding fireworks!

Another interaction that puts the magic into magic milk is the bond between soap molecules and fat and protein molecules. With millions of soap molecules pairing up with millions of fat and protein molecules in the milk, the mixture gets all stirred up. This creates little eruptions in the milk that keep going for several seconds, making a dynamic work of science and art.

MARKER CHROMATOGRAPHY

LEVEL OF DIFFICULTY: EASY
FROM BEGINNING TO END: 20 MINUTES
OTHER CATEGORIES: SCIENCE

? How many different dyes combine to make black ink? This artistic science experiment uses chromatography to separate marker ink into each of its individual dyes. Chromatography is not only used every day in professional chemistry and biology labs, it is also a great way to create cool art.

MATERIALS
- Coffee filter
- Washable markers
- Craft stick
- Binder clip
- Pint-size jar with a couple of inches of water in the bottom
- Paper towel

THE STEPS

1. Use markers to draw a design on a coffee filter. It can be circular or asymmetrical—whatever you feel inspired to draw.

2. Fold the coffee filter in half and then in half again.

3. Attach a craft stick to the top of the coffee filter with a binder clip.

4. Place the coffee filter in the jar of water (suspended by the craft stick) so that the bottom tip is touching the water. Leave it there for a couple of minutes and observe what happens.

5. When the water line reaches the top of the coffee filter, pull it out of the water, unfold it, and let it dry on a paper towel.

Observations What changes did you notice while the coffee filter was suspended in water?

Now Try This! Compare the different bands each marker produces through chromatography. Which marker ink contains the most colors?

The Hows and Whys Marker inks are made from many different colored dyes. This is most obvious with dark colors, such as black and purple. Each dye is made up of different chemicals, some heavier and some lighter, that travel at different rates with the water as it moves them up the paper. The heavier dyes will separate out first and move more slowly, while the lighter dyes keep moving faster up the paper, creating a tie-dyed or washed-out effect.

MAGNET PAINTING

LEVEL OF DIFFICULTY: EASY

FROM BEGINNING TO END: 20 MINUTES

OTHER CATEGORIES: SCIENCE, TECHNOLOGY

? What kind of art can you create with magnets? Experiment with magnetic movement and patterns to design a one-of-a-kind masterpiece.

MATERIALS

- Plastic container
- Paper
- Scissors
- Tempera paint
- Small metal objects from around the house, such as washers, springs, safety pins, screws, and ball bearings
- Magnet

THE STEPS

1. Trim a piece of paper with scissors so that it fits into a plastic container.

2. Dip each metal object into paint and then place it on the paper.

3. Use the magnet to move the metal objects around the paper from underneath the plastic container.

Observations What kinds of patterns does each object produce as it moves around the paper?

Now Try This! Dip other magnets into paint and place them on the paper in the plastic container. Move them around with the magnet underneath the plastic container to create more interesting art. Experiment with the attractive and repulsive forces between magnets.

The Hows and Whys Magnets are strong enough to attract metal objects, even through paper and plastic. Dipping those objects into paint first enables you to see how the objects move with the motion of the magnet.

RAINBOW COLORING

LEVEL OF DIFFICULTY: EASY
FROM BEGINNING TO END: 15 MINUTES
OTHER CATEGORIES: SCIENCE

? Can you create a rainbow in your own home? Learn how rainbows are made in nature and then capture one for yourself.

MATERIALS

- Glass triangular or teardrop prism
- White paper
- Colored pencils

THE STEPS

1. On a sunny day, set the prism in a window that receives a lot of light.

2. Experiment with the angle of the prism to project a rainbow around the room.

3. Angle the rainbow onto a piece of white paper. Use colored pencils to color over the rainbow from the prism.

Observations How does the size and shape of the rainbow change with the angle of the prism?

Now Try This! Take a flashlight, a prism, and a black piece of paper into a dark room. Set the prism on the black paper and shine the light through the prism at different angles. How is it different from sunlight? How is it the same?

The Hows and Whys Nature's prism is a raindrop. Raindrops work the same way a triangular prism does by dispersing white light from the sun, or breaking the light into its visible colors: red, orange, yellow, green, blue, and purple. Each color is refracted at a different angle, creating a rainbow.

OIL AND WATERCOLOR RESISTANT PAINTING

LEVEL OF DIFFICULTY: EASY

FROM BEGINNING TO END: 30 MINUTES

OTHER CATEGORIES: SCIENCE

? Can you create interesting textured art using oil and water? Experiment with mixing oil and watercolors while producing a gorgeous masterpiece.

MATERIALS

- Baking sheet
- White card stock
- Paintbrush
- Cooking oil
- Liquid watercolors

THE STEPS

1. Place the card stock on a baking sheet to catch any mess.

2. Use a paintbrush to paint a design on the paper using the cooking oil. For best results, make it a strong, thick layer.

3. Finish the painting using watercolors.

Observations What do you notice when you paint with watercolors over the oil design? What happens when the painting dries?

Now Try This! What happens if you let the oil dry on the paper first and then paint over it with watercolors? Is it different from trying to paint over fresh oil? Why?

The Hows and Whys Oil and water do not mix because they are made of different kinds of chemical bonds. Oil is made of nonpolar bonds, while water is held together with polar bonds. In this painting, oil repels watercolors. This prevents the watercolors from soaking into the paper and creates a very interesting result.

ICY ART

LEVEL OF DIFFICULTY: EASY
FROM BEGINNING TO END: 20 MINUTES
OTHER CATEGORIES: SCIENCE

(?) What happens when salt is sprinkled onto ice? Not only will you discover the answer to this question, but you will also use the interaction between salt and ice to create interesting and colorful textured art.

MATERIALS

- Bowl full of ice cubes
- Salt
- Liquid watercolors
- Paintbrush

THE STEPS

1. Sprinkle salt onto the ice cubes in the bowl.

2. Wait a few moments and watch how the salt melts tiny tunnels into the ice.

3. Use a paintbrush to color the ice cubes with watercolors.

4. Add more salt to different sides of the ice cubes to create gorgeous textured ice cube art.

Observations Can you see tiny tunnels inside the ice cubes?

Now Try This! Freeze water in large plastic storage containers to start with an even bigger canvas.

The Hows and Whys Under normal conditions, ice melts at 32 degrees Fahrenheit. However, when salt is added, the melting point of ice decreases several degrees. This means that the tiny grains of salt melt tunnels and tracks into the ice. Painting over the texture illuminates these tunnels, creating a unique and beautiful masterpiece.

SCRIBBLE BOT

LEVEL OF DIFFICULTY: MEDIUM
FROM BEGINNING TO END: 30 MINUTES
OTHER CATEGORIES: TECHNOLOGY,
ENGINEERING

? Can you design and build a robot that colors all by itself? You'll be using a mechanical toothbrush, markers, and your own creativity to make your very own scribble bot.

MATERIALS

- Mechanical toothbrush (the inexpensive models from the dollar store work the best)
- 3 washable markers
- Clear tape
- Large piece of white paper

THE STEPS

1. Use clear tape to attach all 3 markers to the motorized end of the mechanical toothbrush. Make sure that the scribble bot stands up on the marker tips like a 3-legged stool.

2. Remove the caps from the markers, set the scribble bot on the paper, and turn on the motor.

3. Watch as your robot draws and skips around the paper, leaving unique patterns behind!

Observations Why does the scribble bot draw the patterns the way that it does? Can you alter that pattern?

Now Try This! You can modify the pattern by adding more markers or changing the height of the markers. Experiment with your robot and see what interesting patterns you can create.

The Hows and Whys When a mechanical toothbrush is turned on, the motor rotates. The rotation creates a force that translates into vibrations you can feel with your hand. Attaching markers to the robot makes it easy to see the patterns the vibrating motion creates.

SYMMETRY PAINTING

LEVEL OF DIFFICULTY: EASY
FROM BEGINNING TO END: 30 MINUTES
OTHER CATEGORIES: MATH

? Symmetry exists in nature all around us: on leaves, flowers, butterflies, and snowflakes. Can you create a work of art that is symmetrical? In addition to painting a masterpiece, you will also work on your geometry skills!

! *Caution:* Painting can get messy. You may want to wear a smock and place some newspaper in your work area to protect your clothes and the table.

MATERIALS

- Large piece of card stock
- Paintbrush
- Tempera paint
- Mirror

THE STEPS

1. Fold the card stock in half and then unfold it.

2. Choose one half of the card stock to paint on.

3. Use a paintbrush to paint a picture or a pattern on that one side. For best results, use a thick layer of paint.

4. Fold the card stock at the crease and press it down hard to transfer the pattern to the other side of the paper.

5. Open the card stock back up to see your symmetrical painting. Verify that it is symmetrical by holding a mirror along the crease line. Does the pattern in the mirror look the same as the pattern behind the mirror?

Observations Did you make any new colors?

Now Try This! Experiment with more symmetry by painting on one quarter of the paper, folding the paper in half one way, unfolding it, and then folding it in half the other way and pressing down. What kinds of patterns are produced this way?

The Hows and Whys When the card stock is folded and the paint is transferred to the other side, it imprints an identical pattern there. When an image is made up of exactly similar parts facing each other, it is symmetrical. This is the same way a mirror reflects an image. The reflection is a symmetrical twin of the original.

SPIN ART

LEVEL OF DIFFICULTY: EASY
FROM BEGINNING TO END: 25 MINUTES
OTHER CATEGORIES: SCIENCE

Can you experiment with rotation and centrifugal force to create a beautiful work of art? Use an unexpected kitchen tool and some paint to produce unique patterns and new colors.

MATERIALS

- Salad spinner
- Coffee filters
- Tempera paint
- Paper towels

THE STEPS

1. Place 2 or 3 coffee filters in a salad spinner.

2. Drip paint onto the coffee filters. Use a variety of colors and drip them in any pattern you wish.

3. Close the salad spinner and give it a good spin.

4. Carefully remove your art from the salad spinner, let it dry on paper towels, and proudly display it!

Observations How did the pattern on the coffee filter change after it was spun in the salad spinner?

Now Try This! Experiment with color mixing by using only primary colors on the coffee filters. How do the colors mix together? What new colors are created?

The Hows and Whys A salad spinner works by rotating a basket very rapidly. When spun around, paint on the coffee filters flies outward from the center because of centrifugal force. This makes the colors mix and gives you a beautiful splat pattern on your masterpiece.

WATER GLASS XYLOPHONE

LEVEL OF DIFFICULTY: EASY

FROM BEGINNING TO END: 20 MINUTES

OTHER CATEGORIES: SCIENCE, MATH

? Can you make a musical instrument out of cups and water? Use the power of math and science to produce your own sound waves and learn how to play your very own water glass xylophone.

MATERIALS

- 8 identical drinking glasses or Mason jars
- Measuring cups
- Water
- Food coloring
- Plastic spoons, wooden spoons, and/or wooden pencils

THE STEPS

1. Arrange the glasses in a straight line.

2. Use measuring cups to add 1¾ cups water to the first glass, 1½ cups water to the second glass, 1¼ cups water to the third glass, and so on, decreasing the amount of water by ¼ cup each time. The last glass should contain no water.

3. Use food coloring to dye the water in each glass a different color.

4. Use a plastic spoon to tap the glasses.

Observations What does each glass sound like when you tap it? Which glasses produce a lower sound? A higher sound?

Now Try This! Experiment with different tappers to see how they produce different sounds. Use a metal spoon, a wooden spoon, or a glass rod. Experiment to figure out how to play a familiar tune on your water glass xylophone, like "Happy Birthday" or "Mary Had a Little Lamb."

The Hows and Whys When you tap on the glasses, a sound wave is produced inside. The pitch of the sound depends on how fast the sound wave travels. Since the glass with the most water slows the sound wave down the most, it produces the lowest pitch. A sound wave in the empty glass has nothing to slow it down, so it travels quickly, producing a higher pitch.

Chapter Six

MATH

Pull out your ruler, roll out your scale, and get ready to measure, calculate, record, and graph like a pro!

In this chapter, you will construct a tall paper chain with a single sheet of paper, make your own sundial to tell time, set off a soda geyser eruption, discover how much air your lungs can hold, and much, much more!

Math is central to every other STEAM field. You need to be able to measure length, distance, output, angles, volume, weight, temperature, and time to know how well your experiments and inventions are working. In order to compare which designs and procedures work the best, you need to know how to measure the results.

Many of experiments in this chapter require the use of tables and graphs. You can either draw your own or photocopy the templates found in the back of this book. Good mathematicians keep copious records and then neatly organize their results on easy-to-read tables and graphs.

Keep in mind that there is always some error involved when taking measurements. It's difficult sometimes to measure distance, time, or volume precisely. Do your best to be accurate, and repeat the activity a few times to average your results together for an even better measurement.

Mathematicians have a few special tools they use to do their job. Some tools you will be using are a ruler, a tape measure, a protractor, measuring cups, a kitchen scale, thermometers, and a stopwatch. Pull out these tools along with some tables, graphs, and a pencil, and you are ready to go.

A few experiments in this chapter require the use of dry ice. You can easily purchase a block of dry ice at a local grocery store, or go to DryIceIdeas.com/retail-locator to find out where dry ice is sold near you. Once you have a block of dry ice, you can use a hammer to break it up into smaller chunks to use in the fun experiments in this chapter.

Above all, have fun experimenting, measuring, and discovering.

HOW FAST CAN YOU RUN?

LEVEL OF DIFFICULTY: EASY

FROM BEGINNING TO END: 20 MINUTES

? How many miles per hour can you run? First make a guess and then head outside with a tape measure and a stopwatch to find out if you run faster or slower than you think you do.

MATERIALS

- Tape measure
- Stopwatch

THE STEPS

1. Head to a place where you will have plenty of room to run. This can be outside at a park or on a long driveway, or it can be inside on a basketball court or in a long hallway.

2. Use the tape measure to measure the distance you will be running in yards. You may need someone to help you hold the tape measure. You can choose how far you want to run, but 15 to 20 yards is probably a good place to start. If you have access to a football field with the yard lines already measured, that would be best.

3. Have somebody use a stopwatch to time how many seconds it takes you to run the set distance. Write down your time.

4. Divide the distance by the time so you have a speed in yards per second.

5. Convert your speed to miles per hour by multiplying by 3,600 and dividing by 1,760. For example, if you run 30 yards in 5 seconds, your speed would be 6 yards per second. Multiply by 3,600 to convert to hours, and divide by 1,760 to convert to miles: You end up with a speed of 12.3 miles per hour.

CONTINUED ➡

Observations Time yourself running this distance several times. Does your speed change with each trial? Why? Can you maintain this speed while running a longer distance?

Now Try This! Hold something heavy, like a gallon of water, while you run. How does this change your speed?

The Hows and Whys Speed is distance traveled per unit of time, or a measure of how fast something is moving. In this experiment, you convert from a speed measured in yards per second to a more relatable speed measured in miles per hour. Multiply by 3,600 to convert from seconds to hours because there are 3,600 seconds in an hour. Divide by 1,760 to convert from yards to miles because there are 1,760 yards in a mile.

PENNY DOME

LEVEL OF DIFFICULTY: EASY
FROM BEGINNING TO END: 15 MINUTES
OTHER CATEGORIES: SCIENCE

? Can you defy gravity? Perform some science magic by creating a water dome on the surface of a penny. Learn what makes this phenomenon happen and count how many drops of water you can squeeze onto a penny's surface. The results may surprise you.

MATERIALS

- Penny
- Cup of water
- Plastic pipette or medicine dropper

THE STEPS

1. Place a penny on a flat surface.

2. Using a pipette, gently squeeze one droplet of water at a time onto the penny.

3. Count how many drops fit on the penny before the dome bursts and all the water spills off.

4. Repeat this experiment several times and keep track of how many drops fit each time. Calculate the average by adding up the total number of drops and dividing it by the number of trials.

Observations If you repeat this experiment, does the number of droplets that fit on the penny change or stay constant? Why?

Now Try This! Gather several pennies together and label them *Penny A*, *Penny B*, *Penny C*, and so on. Keep track on a table how many drops fit on each penny. Perform several trials and figure out the average number of drops that fit onto a penny.

The Hows and Whys Water molecules are attracted to one another very strongly. At the surface, the water molecules are more attracted to one another than they are to the molecules in the air, which makes them form even tighter bonds with one another. This creates a little dome that can be suspended above the rim of the container holding the water. This dome will stay together until the forces of gravity eventually overcome the forces between the water molecules and the water spills over the edge.

COOLING A SODA CAN

LEVEL OF DIFFICULTY: EASY
FROM BEGINNING TO END: 40 MINUTES
OTHER CATEGORIES: SCIENCE

(?) Not many people enjoy drinking warm soda, but sometimes there isn't enough room in the refrigerator for it. What is the fastest way to cool down a warm can of soda? Experiment to find out how well water and air each conduct heat and reward yourself with a cold and refreshing treat at the end.

MATERIALS

- ⊙ Table from the back of the book (page 229)
- ⊙ Pencil
- ⊙ 4 warm cans of soda
- ⊙ Thermometer
- ⊙ Plastic wrap
- ⊙ Rubber bands
- ⊙ Bowl
- ⊙ Cold water
- ⊙ Ice
- ⊙ Graph from the back of the book (page 230)
- ⊙ Markers

THE STEPS

1. Label 5 columns in the table *Time*, *Freezer*, *Refrigerator*, *Ice Water Bath*, and *Control*, in pencil. You will be recording the temperature of the different cans of soda every 5 minutes.

2. Open the cans of soda and measure the temperature of the soda using a thermometer. Record the time as 0 and record the temperature of all 4 cans on the table.

3. Re-cover the top of each can with plastic wrap secured with a rubber band.

4. Fill a bowl with cold water and a few cups of ice.

5. Place one can in the freezer, one can in the refrigerator, and one can in the ice water bath. Leave one can on the counter as the scientific control.

6. Use the thermometer to measure the temperature of the soda in each can every 5 minutes for 30 minutes.

7. Graph the results of your experiment with the horizontal axis labeled *Time* and the vertical axis labeled *Temperature*. Use a different colored marker to graph each can of soda.

Observations Which method worked the fastest to chill a can of soda? Which method yielded the coldest soda at the end of 30 minutes?

Now Try This! What other methods can you think of to cool down a can of soda? Can you wrap a can in a wet towel or point a fan directly at a can? Can you add salt to the ice water bath? Test out several more methods to determine if there is an even faster way to chill a can of soda.

The Hows and Whys Both a freezer and a refrigerator cool objects down by circulating cool air inside. The cool air transfers heat away from the warm can of soda. However, water is a much better heat conductor than air, so heat is able to leave the soda can in the ice water bath much more quickly.

HOW QUICKLY DOES IT COOL?

LEVEL OF DIFFICULTY: EASY
FROM BEGINNING TO END: 40 MINUTES
OTHER CATEGORIES: SCIENCE

? How fast do ice cubes cool down water compared with dry ice? Which kind of ice do you think will cool down the water faster? Which one makes the water colder at the end? Grab a thermometer and find out.

! *Caution: Always wear gloves or use a towel to handle dry ice. It will burn your skin if it is touched directly.* Ask an adult for help.

MATERIALS
- 2 cups or jars
- Cool water
- 2 thermometers
- Table from the back of the book (page 229)
- Pencil
- Kitchen scale
- 2 ounces ice cubes
- 2 ounces dry ice
- Graph from the back of the book (page 230)
- Markers

THE STEPS

1. Fill both cups ¾ full of cool water. Place a thermometer into each cup and let it calibrate for a few minutes.

2. While you are waiting, label 3 columns of your table *Time*, *Dry Ice Water Temperature*, and *Ice Cube Water Temperature*, in pencil. Next, measure 2 ounces of the ice cubes and then dry ice using the scale.

3. Add the ice cubes to one cup and the dry ice to the other. Record the time and the temperature of the water in each cup on your table.

4. Keep the thermometers in the cups and be sure to stir the water around periodically so that the temperature is uniform.

5. Continue to record the temperature of the water in each cup every minute for 10 to 15 minutes.

CONTINUED ➡

6. Graph the results with the horizontal axis labeled *Time* and the vertical axis labeled *Temperature*. Using markers, graph the dry ice water in one color and the ice cube water in another color. Compare how the temperature of each cup of water changed over time.

Observations Which cup of water cooled down the fastest? Which one got the coldest after all the dry ice and ice cubes were gone?

Now Try This! Use larger cups and add 4 ounces of each kind of ice to each cup. Record the temperature every minute for 30 minutes and see how the results compare.

The Hows and Whys Water freezes at 32 degrees Fahrenheit, while dry ice has a surface temperature of −109.3 degrees Fahrenheit. Since dry ice is so much colder, it will cool water down to a lower temperature.

LUNG CAPACITY

LEVEL OF DIFFICULTY: EASY
FROM BEGINNING TO END: 20 MINUTES
OTHER CATEGORIES: SCIENCE, ENGINEERING

? Do you know how much air your lungs can hold? Make your own spirometer to find out. The results may surprise you.

MATERIALS

- 2-liter plastic bottle or a plastic milk jug with cap
- Water
- Large bowl about halfway full of water
- Bendable drinking straw
- Permanent marker
- Measuring cup

THE STEPS

1. Fill up the bottle all the way with water. Place the cap on.

2. Turn the bottle upside down in the bowl of water. With the mouth of the bottle under the water, carefully remove the cap, being careful not to squeeze any water out of the bottle.

3. Push one end of the straw into the neck of the bottle and hold onto the other end above the water.

4. Take a deep breath and blow gently into the straw until your lungs are empty. The air blows into the bottle and pushes water out into the bowl.

5. All the air you breathe out gets trapped at the top of the bottle. Hold the bottle level and make a mark at this point with a permanent marker.

6. To measure how much air you blew into the bottle, take the bottle out of the bowl and fill it with water up to the mark you made. Dump this water into a measuring cup to see how much it is.

CONTINUED ➡

Observations How much air did you blow into the bottle? Does this surprise you?

Now Try This! An average six-year-old's lungs can hold about 1 liter of air, while an adult's lungs can hold 4 to 6 liters. Can you engineer an experiment that adults can do to find out how much air their lungs hold?

The Hows and Whys Air is less dense than water. When you exhale through the straw into the bottle, the air pushes water out of the bottle as it moves to the top. The air pushes out its identical volume of water, so you can measure how much air was in your lungs by calculating how much water was displaced from the bottle.

PAPER CHAIN CHALLENGE

LEVEL OF DIFFICULTY: EASY
FROM BEGINNING TO END: 30 MINUTES
OTHER CATEGORIES: ENGINEERING

? How long of a chain can you make with just one sheet of paper? Can you make a chain that is taller than you? Experiment with geometry and measurement in this fun and simple challenge.

MATERIALS
- Paper
- Scissors
- Tape
- Ruler

THE STEPS

1. Use scissors to cut a piece of paper into strips. Think about how wide and how long you want them to be.

2. Tape the 2 ends of a strip together to make a circle shape.

3. Feed the next strip of paper through the hole in the first circle and tape the 2 ends together to make an interlocking paper chain. Continue with all the strips of paper.

4. When you are out of paper strips, lay the paper chain down on the ground and measure how long it is with a ruler.

5. Take what you learned during this challenge to make a new and improved paper chain that is longer than the first.

CONTINUED →

Observations How long is your paper chain? Does this surprise you? What size strips make the longest paper chain?

Now Try This! Instead of bending the paper strips into circles to make a chain, try taping the strips together from end to end. How long can you make a paper road using just one sheet of paper?

The Hows and Whys Even though you start out with the same-size paper, cutting it into strips of different lengths and widths can dramatically change how long the finished paper chain is.

CRAFT STICK CATAPULT

LEVEL OF DIFFICULTY: MEDIUM
FROM BEGINNING TO END: 40 MINUTES
OTHER CATEGORIES: SCIENCE, ENGINEERING

Can you build a catapult out of simple craft supplies and launch different projectiles across the room? Measure how far each object flies and modify the catapult to maximize this distance.

Caution: *Ask an adult to help with the hot glue gun.*

MATERIALS

- 7 jumbo craft sticks
- 5 rubber bands
- Plastic bottle cap
- Hot glue gun and glue sticks
- Projectiles to launch, such as marshmallows, pom-poms, pencil-top erasers, and cotton balls
- Tape measure
- Table from the back of the book (page 229)

THE STEPS

1. Make a stack of 5 craft sticks and secure them together with a rubber band on each end. This is the fulcrum.

2. Secure the remaining 2 craft sticks to each other on one end with a rubber band. This is the flinger.

3. Wedge the fulcrum halfway between the open ends of the flinger.

4. Loop another rubber band around the closed end of the flinger a couple of times, leaving enough give in the rubber band to loop it once or twice around one end of the fulcrum. Repeat with another rubber band but attach it to the other side of the fulcrum so that the flinger and the fulcrum stay together.

5. Use hot glue to attach a plastic bottle cap to the closed end of the flinger.

6. Place a projectile in the bottle cap. Hold the catapult with one hand and use your other hand to pull down the flinger. Let it go and watch your projectile fly!

7. Measure the distance the projectile flew with a tape measure.

8. Use a table to keep track of how far the catapult launches different items.

Observations Which kind of projectile flies the farthest?

Now Try This! Can you modify the catapult by changing the fulcrum height or the length of the flinger to make it shoot objects farther? Higher? Keep track of the results on your table.

The Hows and Whys A catapult works by storing tension (or potential energy) in the flexed flinger when it is pulled back. This potential energy is converted into kinetic energy as soon as you release the flinger and let it fly forward.

DISAPPEARING ICE

LEVEL OF DIFFICULTY: MEDIUM
FROM BEGINNING TO END: 90 MINUTES
OTHER CATEGORIES: SCIENCE

? Why is dry ice "dry?" Compare dry ice to regular ice cubes by measuring how the weight of each changes over time. Learn about changing states of matter, get an introduction to dry ice, and have some fun.

! *Caution: Always wear gloves or use a towel to handle dry ice. It will burn your skin if it is touched directly.* *Ask an adult for help.*

MATERIALS

- Table from the back of the book (page 229)
- Pencil
- 2 small bowls
- Kitchen scale
- 2 ounces dry ice
- 2 ounces ice cubes
- Graph from the back of the book (page 230)

THE STEPS

1. Label 3 columns in the table *Time, Ice Cubes,* and *Dry Ice,* in pencil.

2. Weigh the empty bowls on a kitchen scale and record their weights.

3. Place the dry ice in one bowl and the ice cubes in the other bowl.

4. Weigh each bowl again and record the weight on the table.

5. Record the weight of each bowl every 15 minutes.

6. Graph the results of how the weight of each substance changed over time. Label the horizontal axis *Time* and the vertical axis *Weight*.

Observations Check again after a couple of hours: what happened to the dry ice? What happened to the ice cubes? How did the weight of each substance change?

Now Try This! Fill up 2 jars with water. Place dry ice in one and ice cubes in the other and measure how the weight of each jar changes over time. Graph your results.

The Hows and Whys Dry ice is solid carbon dioxide. At room temperature, it sublimes to form carbon dioxide gas. Dry ice is "dry" because it doesn't leave any moisture behind. Once all of the dry ice has sublimed, there is nothing left in the bowl.

Compare dry ice with ice cubes by watching how the weight of the ice cubes stays constant over time. This is because the ice cubes are simply melting into water in the bowl.

POPCORN MATH

LEVEL OF DIFFICULTY: EASY
FROM BEGINNING TO END: 10 MINUTES
OTHER CATEGORIES: SCIENCE

? Will the weight of a bag of popcorn change after it is popped? Learn about the law of conservation of mass by measuring the weight of a bag of popcorn before and after it is popped. Plus, enjoy a delicious snack afterward.

MATERIALS

- Bag of microwave popcorn
- Kitchen scale

THE STEPS

1. Use a kitchen scale to weigh a bag of unpopped popcorn. Record the result.

2. Place the bag in the microwave and cook it according to the instructions on the bag.

3. Let the bag cool for a minute or so. Remove it from the microwave and weigh it again.

Observations Did the weight of the bag of popcorn change? Why?

Now Try This! Open the bag and let the steam escape. Now weigh it. Has it changed? Why?

The Hows and Whys The law of conservation of mass states that mass is neither created nor destroyed in a chemical reaction. This means that no matter how the materials change chemically, if the system is closed, the weight will remain the same. In this experiment, was the popcorn bag a completely closed system?

DRY ICE VOLUME

LEVEL OF DIFFICULTY: MEDIUM
FROM BEGINNING TO END: 30 MINUTES
OTHER CATEGORIES: SCIENCE

? How does the volume of dry ice change over time? Compare dry ice with ice cubes to see what happens as they both disappear from a cup of water.

! Caution: *Always wear gloves or use a towel to handle dry ice. It will burn your skin if it is touched directly.* Ask an adult for help.

MATERIALS
- 2 clear jars or cups
- Warm water
- Food coloring
- Colored tape (masking tape, washi tape, or painter's tape)
- ½ cup ice cubes
- ½ cup dry ice
- Measuring cups

THE STEPS

1. Measure 1 cup of warm water into each jar. Drip a few drops of food coloring into each jar to make them different colors.

2. Place a piece of tape on each jar to mark where the water level is.

3. Add the ice cubes to one jar. Place another piece of tape to mark the new water level.

4. Add the dry ice to the other jar. Mark the new water level with a piece of tape.

5. Watch the jars until all of the ice cubes have melted and all of the dry ice has sublimed away.

6. Mark the final water level with tape.

7. Use measuring cups to measure how much water is left in each jar. How do the 2 jars compare?

Observations What differences do you notice between the jar with ice cubes and the jar with dry ice during the experiment? What is the difference in the final water level?

Now Try This! Try this experiment using cold water instead of warm water. How does it change?

The Hows and Whys Ice cubes melt into the water, so they increase the water level in the jar. However, dry ice sublimes and carries some of the water from the jar out with it. (This is the vapor you see.) The water level in the dry ice jar will be slightly lower than it was at the beginning.

What happened to the water level in the ice cube jar between the time the ice cubes were added and when they melted away? Solid water (ice) takes up slightly more area than liquid water does, so you may notice that the water level actually went down as the ice melted.

THE GREENHOUSE EFFECT

LEVEL OF DIFFICULTY: EASY

FROM BEGINNING TO END: 30 MINUTES

OTHER CATEGORIES: SCIENCE

? Why is the inside of a car always so much warmer on a sunny day than the temperature outside? In this simple science experiment, you will learn about the greenhouse effect and be able to measure it on your own.

MATERIALS

- 2 thermometers
- Glass jar with lid
- Table from the back of the book (page 229)
- Pencil
- Watch
- Graph from the back of the book (page 230)
- Markers

THE STEPS

1. Find a sunny spot outside on a warm day.

2. Place both thermometers and the glass jar in the sun and let them warm up for 3 minutes.

3. While you are waiting, label 3 columns on your table in pencil: *Time*, *Control*, and *Greenhouse*.

4. Look at a watch to note the time and record it on the table along with the temperature of both thermometers.

5. Place one of the thermometers inside the jar and close the lid. This is the greenhouse thermometer. The one outside is the scientific control. Make sure the jar and both thermometers are still in direct sunlight.

6. Record the temperature of both thermometers every minute for 10 minutes.

7. Graph the results of how the temperature of both thermometers changed over time. Label the horizontal axis *Time* and the vertical axis *Temperature*. Use a different colored marker to represent each thermometer.

Observations How did the temperature inside the jar change compared with outside? Is there a point at which the temperature inside the jar levels off?

Now Try This! Get another glass jar and put ¼ cup water into each jar. Place a thermometer into each jar. Seal the lid of one jar, but leave the other one open. Leave them both in direct sunlight and see how the temperature changes.

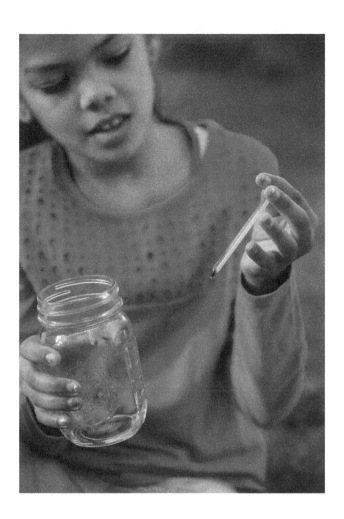

The Hows and Whys The temperature inside the sealed jar rises because light from the sun can get in and warm up the air inside the jar, but the warm air cannot escape. It just keeps getting warmer and warmer. This is the same thing that happens inside a closed car. It is also what happens on Earth and is called the greenhouse effect. Earth's atmosphere traps warm air below, warming the surface to a temperature above what it would be without its atmosphere.

HANGING IN THE BALANCE

LEVEL OF DIFFICULTY: EASY
FROM BEGINNING TO END: 20 MINUTES
OTHER CATEGORIES: ENGINEERING

? Can you make your own simple balance and use it to compare the weight of different objects? Use pennies as a unit of measurement to determine how many pennies each object weighs, and have fun comparing objects from around the house.

MATERIALS

- 2 plastic cups
- Hole puncher
- String
- Scissors
- Plastic or wooden clothes hanger
- Tape
- Objects from around the house to weigh, such as coins, small toys, cereal, and crayons
- Several pennies

THE STEPS

1. Use a hole puncher to punch 2 holes in each cup directly across from each other about 1 inch below the rim.

2. Use scissors to cut 2 pieces of string about 2 feet long.

3. Thread 1 piece of string through the holes in one cup. Loop it over the base of a clothes hanger and tie the string together.

4. Repeat with the other piece of string and the other cup.

5. Adjust the cups so that they are on opposite sides of the hanger.

6. Place the hanger on a doorknob or a level bar for hanging clothes or towels.

7. Adjust the position of the cups on the hanger until the base of the hanger is parallel to the floor. Tape the strings to the hanger so that they don't slide around.

8. Place household objects in the cups and watch what happens. Make a hypothesis about which objects are heavier than others and test them on your hanger balance to see if your hypothesis is correct.

9. Place an object in one cup and then place pennies in the other cup, one by one, until the balance is parallel. Discover how many pennies each object weighs.

Observations How many pennies does each object weigh?

Now Try This! Experiment to see what happens if you shorten the handles on one cup or move one cup toward the center of the hanger.

The Hows and Whys The balance will always tip to the side that holds the heavier object. When the cups hold objects with equal weight, the hanger will be parallel to the ground.

PENCIL SUNDIAL

LEVEL OF DIFFICULTY: EASY
FROM BEGINNING TO END: 8 HOURS
OTHER CATEGORIES: SCIENCE, TECHNOLOGY

Can you construct a clock that will tell time using shadows? Ancient Egyptians were doing this more than 4,500 years ago! Grab a few simple supplies, and make your own sundial.

MATERIALS

- New, unsharpened pencil
- Tape
- Paper plate
- Markers
- Book or full water bottle

THE STEPS

1. Do this experiment on a clear, sunny day. If clouds move in, you may have to try making your sundial a different day.

2. Tape the pencil standing up on its unsharpened, flat end to the center of a paper plate.

3. Find a sunny place outside. Set the paper plate down and trace the pencil's shadow on the paper plate with a marker. Mark the time next to the shadow.

4. Make sure the paper plate and pencil stay in the same position throughout this activity. Place something heavy (like a book or a full water bottle) on part of the paper plate to keep it in place.

5. Each hour on the hour, trace and label the pencil's shadow.

6. Try to get at least 8 shadows traced in a row. The more shadows you capture, the better your sundial will be.

Observations Did the pencil's shadow change its size throughout the day? Why?

Now Try This! Make a human sundial using your own shadow and sidewalk chalk on a large section of asphalt. Head to a driveway, a parking lot, or a playground to trace and measure your shadow each hour, making sure to mark where your feet go so you can stand in the same place each time.

The Hows and Whys As the Earth rotates eastward on its axis, the apparent position of the sun in the sky changes. This makes shadows move across the surface of the Earth.

RACING TO MEASURE

LEVEL OF DIFFICULTY: EASY
FROM BEGINNING TO END: 30 MINUTES
OTHER CATEGORIES: SCIENCE, ENGINEERING

? If you send a toy car down a ramp, at what ramp angle will the car travel the farthest when it hits the ground? Get out your protractor and your tape measure to find out.

MATERIALS

- Cardboard tube from an empty roll of wrapping paper
- Stool or chair
- Toy car
- Tape
- Tape measure
- Table from the back of the book (page 229)
- Pencil
- Protractor
- Graph from the back of the book (page 230)

THE STEPS

1. Set up the cardboard tube on a smooth floor at an angle against a stool or chair. Send a toy car down it like a slide to make sure the chute works.

2. Secure the cardboard tube to the stool with tape.

3. Place the tape measure on the ground with the number 0 at the mouth of the tube. Secure the tape measure so that it stays in place.

4. Prepare a table by labeling 2 columns *Ramp Angle* and *Distance Traveled*, in pencil.

5. Use a protractor to measure the angle between the ramp and the floor. Record it on the table.

6. Send the car down the tube and record the distance it travels. You can send it down several times at the same angle and calculate the average distance it travels for better accuracy.

7. Adjust the angle of the ramp by moving the stool. Record each angle and the distance the car travels with the ramp at that angle.

8. Graph the results at the end with the horizontal axis labeled *Angle* and the vertical axis labeled *Distance*.

Observations What does your graph look like? What ramp angle makes the car travel the farthest on the ground? Does this surprise you?

Now Try This! Send several different kinds of cars down the chute to see which one goes the farthest at each angle. Are there any surprises?

The Hows and Whys A car traveling down a ramp will build up more speed at a steeper angle than it will at a shallow angle. However, once the ramp gets too steep, the car will have a hard time exiting the chute smoothly, so it won't go as far.

SODA GEYSER ERUPTION

LEVEL OF DIFFICULTY: MEDIUM
FROM BEGINNING TO END: 20 MINUTES
OTHER CATEGORIES: SCIENCE

 What happens when Mentos candy is added to diet soda? And why? Get your jogging shoes on and prepare for an impressive soda eruption. At the end, evaluate how big the eruption is by measuring the volume of the soda left over in the bottle. Less soda left over means a bigger eruption.

Caution: *This experiment produces a very big and messy eruption, so be sure to do it outside.*

MATERIALS

- 2-liter bottle of diet soda
- Mentos candy
- Measuring cups

THE STEPS

1. Head outside and place the bottle of soda on a flat surface.

2. Open up the soda, quickly drop in 1 or 2 Mentos, and run away!

3. When the geyser is done erupting, use measuring cups to see how much soda is left behind in the bottle.

Observations What is the soda like after the eruption? How much is left in the bottle?

Now Try This! Repeat this experiment with different kinds of soda and different kinds and amounts of candy to see how you can create the biggest eruption. Measure the soda left behind each time to see which combination works to create the biggest eruption. What other kinds of candy do you think would make a soda geyser?

The Hows and Whys Similar to the Dancing Raisins experiment (page 7), the soda erupts in an impressive column of foam because of the nucleation sites found on the rough surface of the Mentos candy. These are tiny holes on the candy surface that bubbles of carbon dioxide attach to.

When a bottle of soda is opened, some of the carbon dioxide bubbles escape. However, millions more bubbles are stuck in the soda and can't escape out the top because they are too tiny to work their way up through the soda. When a Mentos candy is added, millions of tiny bubbles form on the surface of the Mentos, forming bigger bubbles that can escape. With such a huge rush of bubbles flying out of the bottle at once, the soda gets pushed out, too, creating an exciting, foamy eruption!

The 2 additives in diet soda are important, too. Aspartame and potassium benzoate make it easier for gas bubbles to form in the soda, causing a faster, more explosive geyser to shoot out the top.

Chapter Seven

PUTTING IT ALL TOGETHER

You made it! You have explored the fields of Science, Technology, Engineering, Art, and Math, and you have completed experiments in each one. What new things have you learned and discovered?

Use the activities in this book as a launching pad to a lifelong habit of following the scientific method to discover new things. Ask lots of questions. Wonder why and how and what and when. Learn to love the process of discovery.

By now you are familiar with how the STEAM fields overlap and interconnect. By doing the experiments, you learned that you can't have one field without many others. They enhance one another and build on one another.

There are hundreds of educational and vocational fields that need innovative people who will discover, create, build, and develop the next generation of amazing technological inventions. If you use the skills you have learned in this book, you can be one of those people.

Maybe you will be a scientist. You could work in a biochemistry lab to find a cure for cancer, or you could be the scientist who discovers life on Mars. You could be a field biologist who studies rare jungle animals or a volcanologist who travels the world to study volcanoes.

Maybe you will be a programmer or a hardware engineer. You could develop a new app that helps people or a new game that is fun to play. You could be on a team that invents a new electronic device or improves an old one. Maybe you will develop a new electrical panel for a fighter jet or produce a medical device that saves thousands of lives.

Maybe you will be an engineer. Perhaps you will make a streamlined rocket ship or a hovering car. You could end world hunger by developing a new, inexpensive process to make nutritious food, or you could build strong buildings and bridges that will withstand the forces of nature.

Whatever inventions you develop, you will need to think about how to design them so that they are intuitive, user-friendly, and visually appealing. You will use your creativity, your imagination, and your artistic talents to make sure that people can use your discoveries in the way they are meant to be used.

Perhaps your path will lead you away from the STEAM fields and into the humanities, politics, or music. You could be a teacher, a writer, a rock star, or a lawyer. Whatever your passion, knowing how to question, knowing how to discover, and loving to learn will set you up for success.

Keep exploring. Keep experimenting. Use the ideas in this book to think of ideas of your own. Never stop learning!

Glossary

acceleration: The rate at which something increases its velocity, or how quickly it speeds up.

acid: A molecule that can donate a proton in a chemical reaction.

adhesion: The attraction that holds two different substances together.

air resistance: The frictional force air exerts against a moving object.

angular momentum: The quantity of rotation of a body.

atom: The smallest unit of a chemical element. Each atom consists of a nucleus, which has a positive charge, and a set of electrons that move around the nucleus.

base: A molecule that can accept a proton in a chemical reaction.

buoyancy: The upward force exerted on an object by a fluid that enables the object to float.

capillary action: The ability of water to move against gravity in narrow spaces.

carbon dioxide: A colorless, odorless gas with a density about 60% higher than that of air.

catalyst: A substance that increases the rate of a chemical reaction.

centrifugal force: An apparent force that acts outward on a body moving around a center.

chemical: Any basic substance that is used in or produced by a reaction involving changes to atoms or molecules.

chemical bond: The attraction between atoms.

chemical reaction: A process by which one or more substances are converted into a different product.

chromatography: A technique used to separate the components of a chemical mixture by moving the mixture along a stationary material.

closed circuit: A complete electrical connection around which current flows or circulates.

cohesion: The attraction that holds two molecules of the same substance together.

conductivity: A measure of the ability of a material to conduct heat or an electric current.

conductor: A material, such as metal, through which heat or electricity transfers easily.

crystal: A solid substance whose atoms or molecules are arranged in a highly ordered, geometrical, symmetrical pattern.

density: The degree of compactness of a substance.

dispersion: The separation of white light into colors, or the separation of any radiation according to wavelength.

electric circuit: A closed loop in which electrons continuously flow.

electromagnet: A temporary magnet that is activated by electricity.

electron: A stable subatomic particle with a negative electrical charge found in all atoms.

exothermic reaction: A chemical reaction that gives off heat.

focal point: The point at which light rays meet after refraction.

force: A push or pull on an object.

freezing point: The temperature at which a liquid changes to a solid.

frequency: The number of crests of a wave that move past a given point in a given unit of time.

friction: The resistance that one surface or object encounters when moving over another.

fulcrum: The point or support on which a lever turns.

fungus: A microscopic spore-producing organism that feeds on organic matter.

germinate: When a seed begins to grow and put out shoots.

gravity: The pulling force exerted by Earth.

inertia: The resistance of an object to a change in its state of motion.

insulator: A material, such as plastic, wood, or rubber, that does not readily allow the passage of heat, sound, or electricity.

kinetic energy: The energy an object has because of its motion.

lift: The force that directly opposes the weight of an airborne object and holds it in the air.

magnetism: A physical force created by electric currents.

mass: The measurement of how much matter is in an object.

melting point: The temperature at which a solid changes to a liquid.

molecule: A group of atoms bonded together to make a chemical compound.

momentum: The force a moving object possesses, expressed as the product of its mass multiplied by its velocity.

neutron: A subatomic particle of about the same mass as a proton but without an electric charge, present in all atomic nuclei except those of ordinary hydrogen.

non-Newtonian fluid: A liquid whose viscosity changes when a stress or a force is applied.

nonpolar bond: A bond between atoms or molecules in which electrons are shared equally.

nucleation sites: Small holes or uneven surfaces that assist the physical separation of solids, liquids, and gases.

nucleus: The positively charged central core of an atom, consisting of protons and neutrons and containing nearly all its mass.

open circuit: An electric circuit in which the normal path of current has been interrupted.

oxidation: A chemical reaction in which an atom, molecule, or ion gives up electrons, often by combining with oxygen.

pendulum: A weight suspended from a pivot so that it can swing freely.

photosynthesis: The process by which plants use sunlight to make their food from carbon dioxide and water.

pitch: The degree of highness or lowness of a tone.

polar bond: A bond between atoms or molecules in which electrons are shared unequally, creating partially charged positive and negative areas.

polymer: A long chain of molecules.

potential energy: Mechanical or stored energy from an object that comes from factors such as its position relative to others, internal stress, or electric charge.

pressure: The continuous physical force exerted on or against an object by something in contact with it.

projectile: An object thrown or shot forward by the exertion of a force.

proton: An elementary particle with a positive charge, found in the nucleus of an atom.

reflection: The return of light or sound waves from a surface.

refraction: The bending of light when it passes from one medium into another medium with a different density.

resistance: A force that opposes motion or the flow of electricity.

rotational inertia: The property by which a rotating body maintains its state of uniform rotational motion.

scientific control: An untreated sample that lets you see what normally happens.

solute: A substance that is dissolved into another substance.

solution: A mixture of two or more substances, usually a solute dissolved in a solvent.

solvent: A liquid that dissolves another substance to form a solution.

speed: Distance traveled per unit of time.

spirometer: An instrument for measuring the air capacity of the lungs.

static electricity: An electric charge produced by friction.

sublimation: The phase transition of a substance from a solid directly to a gas.

supersaturated solution: A solution that contains more of the dissolved material than could be dissolved by the solvent under normal circumstances.

surface tension: The attraction between molecules on the surface of a liquid that causes it to form into droplets.

symmetry: The property of being made up of exactly similar parts facing one another or around an axis.

temperature: The degree of heat present in an object.

thrust: The force that moves an airborne object through the air.

trajectory: The curved path followed by a flying object.

variable: Something you can change in an experiment.

velocity: The speed of something in a specific direction.

viscous: Having a thick, sticky consistency that does not flow easily.

vortex: A mass of whirling fluid or air.

wavelength: The distance between successive crests of a wave.

Resources

Below you will find websites that contain hundreds of STEAM activities, lessons, free resources, and ideas.

WEBSITES

ScienceKiddo.com
STEAM experiments with free printable science journal pages.

ScienceKids.co.nz
Fun science experiments, cool facts, online games, free activities, ideas, lesson plans, photos, quizzes, videos, and science fair projects.

DeceptivelyEducational.blogspot.com
STEAM games, activities, and resources.

ScienceBuddies.org
Science fair project ideas for kids and STEM lesson plans for educators.

FrugalFun4Boys.com
Technology and engineering activities that are simple and inexpensive to do.

Exploratorium.edu/snacks
Hands-on science activities that teachers or students can make using common, inexpensive, and readily available materials.

Tinkering.Exploratorium.edu/projects
A hands-on tinkering website for playful invention and investigation.

ScientificAmerican.com/education/bring-science-home
Fun science activities that parents and their kids can do together in a half hour or less using household items.

ScienceBob.com
Science experiments and science fair project ideas.

SteveSpanglerScience.com/lab/experiments
Impressive STEAM projects and ideas.

Education.com/science-fair
A vast collection of science fair project ideas written by science teachers, professional scientists, and educational consultants on popular science fair topics ranging from physics and chemistry to biology and even sociology, suitable for every grade level.

BioEdOnline.org/lessons-and-more
National standard–aligned, high-quality lessons, teacher guides, slides, videos, and supplemental materials.

Table

Graph

Experiment Index

Index

Acknowledgments

This book could not have been produced without the valuable help and support of so many.

First and foremost, thank you to my three children, who are my inspiration for everything I do. I wrote this book with you in mind. Thank you for being my muses, for putting up with lots of free time while I've been writing, and for encouraging me and keeping me on track. Above all, thank you, all three of you, for consistently sleeping through the night this past month.

Thank you to my husband, Ben, who has been my rock throughout this process. Thank you for outlining a schedule for me, for picking up the slack around the house, for kicking me out of bed at 5:00 a.m. to work, for being my number one cheerleader, and for taking the kids out on adventures so I could write.

I appreciate the support of so many friends and family members who have checked in with me on my progress, who have celebrated with me after meeting my deadlines, and who have given our family an extra dose of love and encouragement. Thank you for understanding when I have been slow to return phone calls, texts, and emails. You know I love you all.

Last, but not least, a big thanks to my editor, Susan Randol, and to the staff at Callisto Media. Thank you so much for the opportunity to work with you to produce this amazing book. I appreciate your guidance, your patience, and your brilliant ideas. Thank you for making my dream a reality.

About the Author

Crystal Chatterton is a homeschooling mom of three. After trading an academic career in chemistry to stay home with her kids, she launched her website, ScienceKiddo.com, to focus on sharing her love of STEAM with thousands of children around the world. She lives in Portland, Oregon, with her husband and kids.